The
Enlightenment

Titles in the World History Series

The Age of Augustus
The Age of Exploration
The Age of Feudalism
The Age of Napoleon
The Age of Pericles
The Alamo
America in the 1960s
The American Frontier
The American Revolution
Ancient Greece
The Ancient Near East
Architecture
Aztec Civilization
The Battle of the
    Little Bighorn
The Black Death
The Byzantine Empire
Caesar's Conquest of Gaul
The California Gold Rush
The Chinese Cultural
    Revolution
The Civil Rights Movement
The Collapse of the
    Roman Republic
The Conquest of Mexico
The Crimean War
The Crusades
The Cuban Missile Crisis
The Cuban Revolution
The Early Middle Ages
Egypt of the Pharaohs
Elizabethan England
The End of the Cold War
The Enlightenment
The French and Indian War
The French Revolution
The Glorious Revolution
The Great Depression
Greek and Roman
    Mythology
Greek and Roman Science

Greek and Roman Sport
Greek and Roman Theater
The History of Slavery
Hitler's Reich
The Hundred Years' War
The Industrial Revolution
The Inquisition
The Italian Renaissance
The Late Middle Ages
The Lewis and Clark
    Expedition
The Mexican Revolution
The Mexican War of
    Independence
Modern Japan
The Mongol Empire
The Persian Empire
Prohibition
The Punic Wars
The Reformation
The Relocation of the
    North American Indian
The Renaissance
The Roaring Twenties
The Roman Empire
The Roman Republic
Roosevelt and the New
    Deal
The Russian Revolution
Russia of the Tsars
The Scientific Revolution
The Spread of Islam
The Stone Age
The Titanic
Traditional Africa
Traditional Japan
The Travels of Marco Polo
Twentieth Century Science
The Wars of the Roses
The Watts Riot
Women's Suffrage

WORLD
HISTORY SERIES ■■■

The
Enlightenment

by
John M. Dunn

Lucent Books, P.O. Box 289011, San Diego, CA 92198-9011

Library of Congress Cataloging-in-Publication Data

Dunn, John M., 1949–
    The Enlightenment / by John M. Dunn.
        p.   cm.—(World history series)
    Includes bibliographical references and index.
    Summary: Discusses various aspects of the Enlightenment
including its roots, philosophes, attacks on Christianity, revolt
against reason, campaigns to reform society, and legacy.
    ISBN 1-56006-242-8 (lib. : alk. paper)
    1. Eighteenth century—Juvenile literature. 2. Enlighten-
ment—Juvenile literature. 3. Europe—History—18th century—
Juvenile literature [1. Enlightenment. 2. Eighteenth century. 3.
Europe—History—18th century.] I. Title. II. Series.
D286.D86 1999
940.2'53—dc21   98-8373
                                                           CIP
                                                            AC

Contents

Foreword

Each year on the first day of school, nearly every history teacher faces the task of explaining why his or her students should study history. One logical answer to this question is that exploring what happened in our past explains how the things we often take for granted—our customs, ideas, and institutions—came to be. As statesman and historian Winston Churchill put it, "Every nation or group of nations has its own tale to tell. Knowledge of the trials and struggles is necessary to all who would comprehend the problems, perils, challenges, and opportunities which confront us today." Thus, a study of history puts modern ideas and institutions in perspective. For example, though the founders of the United States were talented and creative thinkers, they clearly did not invent the concept of democracy. Instead, they adapted some democratic ideas that had originated in ancient Greece and with which the Romans, the British, and others had experimented. An exploration of these cultures, then, reveals their very real connection to us through institutions that continue to shape our daily lives.

Another reason often given for studying history is the idea that lessons exist in the past from which contemporary societies can benefit and learn. This idea, although controversial, has always been an intriguing one for historians. Those who agree that society can benefit from the past often quote philosopher George Santayana's famous statement, "Those who cannot remember the past are condemned to repeat it." Historians who subscribe to Santayana's philosophy believe that, for example, studying the events that led up to the major world wars or other significant historical events would allow society to chart a different and more favorable course in the future.

Just as difficult as convincing students to realize the importance of studying history is the search for useful and interesting supplementary materials that present historical events in a context that can be easily understood. The volumes in Lucent Books' World History Series attempt to present a broad, balanced, and penetrating view of the march of history. Ancient Egypt's important wars and rulers, for example, are presented against the rich and colorful backdrop of Egyptian religious, social, and cultural developments. The series engages the reader by enhancing historical events with these cultural contexts. For example, in *Ancient Greece*, the text covers the role of women in that society. Slavery is discussed in *The Roman Empire*, as well as how slaves earned their freedom. The numerous and varied aspects of everyday life in these and other societies are explored in each volume of the series. Additionally, the series covers the major political, cultural, and philosophical ideas as the torch of civilization is passed from ancient Mesopotamia and Egypt, through Greece, Rome, Medieval Europe, and other world cultures, to the modern day.

The material in the series is formatted in a thorough, precise, and organized manner. Each volume offers the reader a comprehensive and clearly written overview of an important historical event or period. The topic under discussion is placed in a broad, historical context. For example, *The Italian Renaissance* begins with a discussion of the High Middle Ages and the loss of central control that allowed certain Italian cities to develop artistically. The book ends by looking forward to the Reformation and interpreting the societal changes that grew out of the Renaissance. Thus, students are not only involved in an historical era, but also enveloped by the events leading up to that era and the events following it.

One important and unique feature in the World History Series is the primary and secondary source quotations that richly supplement each volume. These quotes are useful in a number of ways. First, they allow students access to sources they would not normally be exposed to because of the difficulty and obscurity of the original source. The quotations range from interesting anecdotes to far-sighted cultural perspectives and are drawn from historical witnesses both past and present. Second, the quotes demonstrate how and where historians themselves derive their information on the past as they strive to reach a consensus on historical events. Lastly, all of the quotes are footnoted, familiarizing students with the citation process and allowing them to verify quotes and/or look up the original source if the quote piques their interest.

Finally, the books in the World History Series provide a detailed launching point for further research. Each book contains a bibliography specifically geared toward student research. A second, annotated bibliography introduces students to all the sources the author consulted when compiling the book. A chronology of important dates gives students an overview, at a glance, of the topic covered. Where applicable, a glossary of terms is included.

In short, the series is designed not only to acquaint readers with the basics of history, but also to make them aware that their lives are a part of an ongoing human saga. Perhaps they will then come to the same realization as famed historian Arnold Toynbee. In his monumental work, *A Study of History*, he wrote about becoming aware of history flowing through him in a mighty current, and of his own life "welling like a wave in the flow of this vast tide."

Important Dates in the History of the Enlightenment

1350	1375	1400	1425	1450	1475	1500	1525	1550	1575

1350

Renaissance begins in Italy.

1519

Martin Luther starts Protestant Revolution.

1624

Lord Herbert of Cherbury publishes *De veritate*.

1682

Pierre Bayle launches the *News of the Republic of Letters*.

1687

Edmund Halley publishes Issac Newton's *Principia Mathematica*.

1688–1689

The Glorious Revolution is under way.

1690

John Locke publishes *Two Treatises of Government*.

1697

Pierre Bayle publishes *Historical and Critical Dictionary*.

1711

Joseph Addison and Richard Steele's *Spectator* appears.

1717

Society of Freemasons is established.

1719

Daniel Defoe publishes *Robinson Crusoe*.

1720

John Toland publishes *Reasons for Naturalising the Jews in Great Britain and Ireland*.

1726

Voltaire flees to England.

1734

Voltaire publishes *Letters on the English Nation*.

1739

David Hume publishes *A Treatise of Human Nature*.

1747

Julien Offroy de La Mettrie publishes *L'Homme-machine (Man a Machine)*.

1748

Baron de La Brède et de Montesquieu publishes *The Spirit of Laws*.

1749

Jean-Jacques Rousseau publishes "Has the Progress of the Sciences and Arts Contributed to the Corruption or to the Improvement of Human Conduct?"; Henry Fielding publishes *Tom Jones*.

1751

First volume of the *Encyclopedia* appears.

1754

Rousseau publishes "Discourse on the Origin of Inequality Among Men."

1600	1625	1650	1675	1700	1725	1750	1775	1800	1809

1760

The Illuminati is founded; Laurence Sterne's *Tristram Shandy* is published.

1761

Rousseau publishes *La Nouvelle Heloise.*

1762

Rousseau publishes *Emile* and *The Social Contract.*

1764

Cesare Beccaria publishes *An Essay on Crimes and Punishments.*

1770

Baron d'Holbach publishes *A System of Nature.*

1771

Catholic Church counters philosophes with the *Encyclopedia methodisque.*

1776

Declaration of Independence is proclaimed; American Revolution begins; Adam Smith publishes *The Wealth of Nations;* Sturm und Drang is under way; Edward Gibbon publishes *The Decline and Fall of the Roman Empire.*

1781

Immanuel Kant publishes *Critique of Pure Reason.*

1783

United States wins independence from Great Britain; Austria's Joseph II decrees religious toleration; Pietro Tambirini publishes *On Ecclesiastical and Civil Toleration.*

1784

John and Charles Wesley establish Methodist Church.

1787

The U.S. Constitution is adopted.

1789

The Bill of Rights is ratified and added to U.S. Constitution; French Revolution begins; French National Assembly adopts the Declaration of the Rights of Man and the Citizen.

1791

France adopts a new constitution; Olympe de Gouges issues "Declaration of the Rights of Woman."

1793–1794

Reign of Terror in France.

1794

French Revolution ends.

1804

Napoléon declared emperor of France.

1809

Inquisition ends in Italy.

Casting Light upon Darkness

The Enlightenment was a period of intense intellectual ferment that lasted from approximately A.D. 1650 to 1789. More a spirit than an organized movement, its overriding goal was to cast the light of understanding on the darkness of humanity's ignorance, selfishness, and foolishness.

England was the cradle of the Enlightenment, but France was the land of its maturity. Eventually it spread to other countries, including America, where more than anywhere else its goals were realized.

Although many contributed to this historic crusade, its best-known leaders were the French thinkers, writers, politicians, merchants, nobles, revolutionaries, and theologians called philosophes.

In the Enlightenment's early days, most philosophes championed the power of human reason and the scientific method—rather than faith, emotion, loyalty, superstition, and obedience to authority—as the best tools to solve vexing social, economic, and political problems. Many agreed with eighteenth-century English writer Lord Chesterfield's advice: "Consult your reason betimes: I do not say it will always prove an unerring guide, for human reason is not infallible; but it will prove the best guide you can follow."[1]

Almost everything was fair game for these disciples of reason. What society worked best? they wondered. Why were so many laws unjust and cruel? How did the universe operate? Was there a God? Was the earth really only four thousand years old as some theologians claimed? Were there natural laws that governed human affairs? Could they be understood by the rational human mind? Who had the power to govern? How did the human mind work? Could it be trusted to inform humanity about the real world? If not, could humans ever know anything?

More than curiosity motivated the advocates of enlightenment. Many despised Europe's monarchies and accused rulers of using their subjects as pawns in dangerous power-grabbing games. The philosophes also resented the class of landowning nobles, who clung to centuries-old customs that gave them an unfair share of power, prestige, special privileges, and tax exemptions at the expense of the majority.

But the proponents of enlightenment directed their greatest ire at organized religion, especially the Catholic Church, which many believed abused entire populations through fear, intimidation, threats, and false knowledge.

God ceased to be an important force in the lives of many thinkers of the Enlightenment. As never before, men and women of the eighteenth century found themselves guided by self-interest and their own conscience. "Instead of waiting upon the Second Coming of Christ, Reason boldly essayed the task of saving mankind from all the miseries, crimes, and follies of the past,"[2] writes historian William H. McNeil.

Like any new campaign that seeks to bring about massive social change, the Enlightenment spawned an array of critics and enemies. A counterforce to the philosophes materialized. Across Europe, religious and government leaders denounced and persecuted philosophes and accused them of treason, anarchy, and atheism.

Critics also emerged within the ranks of the Enlightenment itself. Dissenters charged that the use of reason failed to explain all. There was, they argued, also room for faith, emotion, and sentiment in the human heart.

This new interest in human sentiment did not weaken the movement. It merely broadened it by adding a humanitarian impulse. Together reason and feeling did much to eradicate brutality and injustice. Superstition faded. The ancient practice of burning witches ended. Most countries in Europe rid themselves of slavery and torture. Authorities made fairer laws. Philosophes succeeded in laying the groundwork for more humane treatment of women, children, and minorities. They also greatly diminished the power of monarchs,

Two men enter into a scholarly disagreement. During the Enlightenment, educated men tried to use reason to understand the world.

Eighteenth-century chemists work in an early laboratory. Unlike medieval thinkers, Enlightenment philosophes tried to test scientific theories with experiments, eliminating superstition.

popes, and priests and gave birth to the idea of human rights for all human beings.

Finally, the philosophes also successfully changed the way millions of people thought about religion, economics, politics, psychology, literature, art, music, science, manners, and even the nature of reality. They also helped set the stage for democratic revolutions in America and France.

Despite these lasting achievements, critics of the Enlightenment insist that the irreverence and skepticism unleashed by the philosophes severely undermined the social order and contributed to murderous mob rule brought on by the French Revolution. They also argue that the Enlightenment paved the way for a cold, materialistic, and godless modern world in which millions of people find themselves living purposeless, lost, alienated lives.

For better and for worse, the Enlightenment was a turning point in history that ushered in the contemporary age. As historian Louis Bredvold puts it, "In a word, the Enlightenment was the period when Europe really emerged from the Middle Ages and the Modern Mind was born."[3]

Chapter

1 The Roots of the Enlightenment

"Do we now live in an *enlightened age?*" Immanuel Kant, the famous German philosopher, once asked. "The answer is 'No, but we do live in an *age of enlightenment.*'"[4]

Like many other thinkers in Europe and America, Kant believed that his age—the eighteenth century—was characterized by an intense human desire to know the truth. "The eighteenth century is perhaps the last period in the history of Western Europe when . . . [the ability of the human mind to know everything] . . . was thought to be an attainable goal,"[5] writes Enlightenment scholar Isaiah Berlin.

Much of this quest for knowledge was the product of a historical trend set in motion centuries earlier. But there was also a practical side to it. By now, many Europeans were convinced that knowledge, truth, and other forms of enlightenment were all needed to overhaul a corrupt and unjust society that benefited monarchs, nobles, and clergymen at the expense of others.

The roots of the Age of Enlightenment stretch back to the Renaissance, a rebirth in learning that began about A.D. 1350 after centuries of relatively slow—if not stagnant—intellectual growth during Europe's

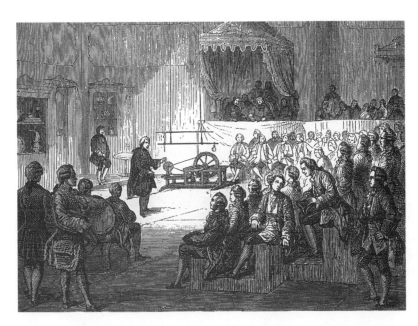

Men attend a course in physics at the College of Navarre in France in 1754. The Enlightenment brought about an increased desire to learn about the world and improve oneself through study.

Middle Ages. In contrast, the Renaissance was an era that emphasized study, learning, and self-improvement. Its thinkers, writers, and artists proudly "rediscovered" the classic literature of the Greeks and Romans that had been ignored or forgotten during the Middle Ages. But gifted individuals of the Renaissance also created original works in literature, art, and architecture and laid down the foundations of modern science.

At the time, new printing presses with movable type made it possible to transmit the ideas of the Renaissance farther, faster, and more cheaply than ever before. Previously all books were made entirely by hand, a time-consuming and expensive process.

Exploration of the world also contributed to the rise of the Enlightenment. From the Renaissance on, fleets of European ships set sail to explore unknown areas of the world. The tales returning sailors told of human life in distant exotic lands sparked an intense European interest in other cultures and forced comparisons with their own societies.

Meanwhile, the intellectual mood of the Renaissance spawned a growing skepticism of the teachings of the Catholic Church, the institution that dominated religious life in Europe. Many critics openly made fun of corrupt and immoral practices within the church; they also questioned church doctrines such as the Trinity, a church teaching that God is three essences in one. Desiderius Erasmus, a Dutch humanist, foreshadowed future skeptics in his book *Familiar Colloquies*, in which he attacked the veneration of religious relics, such as that of the Virgin Mary.

In 1519, Martin Luther, a German monk, launched a protest against church abuses that crescendoed into a massive revolt known as the Protestant Reformation. Through the sixteenth and seventeenth centuries, Catholics and Protestants waged war against one another in the name of God. This bloodletting eventually weakened the authority of the Catholic Church, but it also disillusioned many Christians on both sides. How could it be true, as their spiritual leaders asserted, that each religion was the one true faith? Whose interpretation of the Bible was correct? And did the church really have God's blessing when it persecuted those who disagreed with church authority?

These questions motivated scholars, along with laypersons and religious leaders, to scrutinize and question both the Bible and church pronouncements as never before.

The Scientific Revolution

By the seventeenth century, western Europe found itself in the midst of an exciting era known as the Scientific Revolution that evolved from a spirit of inquiry ignited by the Renaissance. New inventions now existed that enabled scientists to see amazing new worlds. Microscopes, for instance, exposed miniature forms of life never before seen or imagined. Astronomers, meanwhile, gazed through telescopes and wondered at magnified images of distant planets and other celestial bodies of the night. This revolution also made great strides in other fields such as anatomy, modern chemistry, optics, physics, and medicine.

All these breakthroughs utilized a new approach to learning called the scientific

Freedom to Think

Radical German theologian Carl Friedrich Bahrdt endured censorship and criticism from church officials for expressing enlightened views such as the following, quoted in What Is Enlightenment? *edited by James Schmidt.*

"Freedom to think and to judge independently from authority, independently from the pronouncements of the priests, monks, popes, church councils, the Church—this is the holiest, most important, most inviolable right of man. Men have cause to treasure it more highly than all other liberties and rights, because its loss does not merely reduce their happiness, but completely destroys it; because the absence of the freedom makes the perfection of their immortal souls impossible. . . . [W]ithout this right and its exercise they become miserable slaves, and they risk their souls and salvation when they leave it to those to whom they renounced their reason in blind imitation, whether they want to lead them to truth or falsehood, to heaven or to hell.

I call this freedom a right, and indeed an inviolable right, that God has given you, and that no man can or should take from you."

method—an approach based on the use of observation and experimentation—popularized by Francis Bacon, a seventeenth-century English philosopher.

As science relentlessly exposed the secrets of nature, disturbing new questions arose about traditional beliefs. Astronomy, for instance, revealed that the earth was not the center of the universe, as the church had maintained for centuries. Instead it was but one planet that revolved around the sun, itself but a dot among an infinity of suns. This discovery led some thinkers to suggest that contrary to church teaching, humanity was not the measure of all things after all.

If the church—which proclaimed to be God's official communicator on earth and incapable of error—was wrong about the importance of earth, many Europeans wondered, could it be mistaken about other things?

The Importance of Sir Isaac Newton

Ironically, the work of a devout Christian and a brilliant thinker, Sir Isaac Newton, served as a catalyst for the Enlightenment. A professor of mathematics at Cambridge University in England, Newton produced scientific observations and experiments that stunned people around the world. In the previous century, other scientists, such

Sir Isaac Newton's scientific theories propelled the Enlightenment forward. Because Newton's laws dictated that the universe was an ordered place, people believed that the natural world worked on knowable principles.

as Italy's Galileo, had also made revolutionary discoveries only to have their work suppressed by the church. But by Newton's age, the church's grip had weakened considerably and scientists and thinkers felt freer to express their ideas.

In his book *Principia Mathematica*, published in 1687, Newton produced calculations that showed the force of gravity acted uniformly throughout the universe. The same power that attracted planets towards the sun also pulled objects to the ground on earth. In addition, he mathematically determined the gravitational pull one body exerts on another, whether on earth or in outer space. He also originated formulas that could be used to determine the force and speed of bodies in motion, no matter where they were in the universe.

Through his writings, Newton presented the notion that the universe was not a vast unfathomable riddle. Rather, it

appeared to function with machinelike precision that obeyed unchanging laws of nature. And these laws, his work suggested, could be understood with human logic and observation.

Newton's ideas revolutionized human thought. Quite suddenly, someone had come up with an explanation that accounted for the behavior of all matter in the universe as a unified whole. The eighteenth-century English poet Alexander Pope praised Newton's breakthrough with these words:

> Nature and Nature's laws lay hid in night.
>
> God said, let Newton be! and all was light.[6]

Not only did Newton's ideas expand scientific understanding, they also served as a bridge from the Scientific Revolution to the Enlightenment. Inspired by Newton's ability to find underlying causes to the world of matter, a new generation of thinkers began to wonder if a similar approach could be used to uncover other mysteries. If reason could yield facts about the universe, they speculated, why could it not also be used to understand and solve humanity's social, economic, and political problems?

The Ideas of John Locke

A pioneer of such thinking was John Locke, a highly respected English scholar and philosopher. Through his writings, Locke contributed many ideas that established the intellectual foundation for the Enlightenment. Like several other thinkers of his day, he believed in the existence of "natural law." According to his theory, just as laws of nature governed the forces of gravity and magnetism, other laws regulated human behavior. But these are not the laws crafted by legislators in parliaments and town halls. Instead, they are rules that are understandable through the use of reason.

According to Locke, all humans possess the power of reason; and reason itself reveals that all humans have the same natural rights to seek life, liberty, and property. At the same time, they also have the same responsibility not to intrude on the rights of others. "Reason . . . teaches all mankind who will but consult it, that being all equal and independent, no one ought to harm another in his life, health, liberty or possession,"[7] Locke argues.

In *Two Treatises of Government,* published in 1690, Locke unveiled his thinking on political matters. He argued that individuals should be able to use the principles of natural law as a guide to living without a central governing authority. But because they differ in their interpretations of these natural laws, they must agree to

John Locke believed that people were born with the ability to reason and that their reason would guide them to understand and live by certain inalienable rights. He pioneered the idea that a government should take its powers from the people.

adhere to a larger "social contract." This contract obliges people to create a government and give it limited powers to care for the common good. Although individuals must give up some of their freedom, in

Three Laws That Changed the World

Isaac Newton's famous three laws of motion, as worded in Bartlett's Famous Quotations, *revolutionized scientific thinking and helped launch the Enlightenment.*

"1) Every body continues in its state of rest, or of uniform motion in a . . . [straight] line, unless it is compelled to change that state by forces impressed upon it.
2) The change of motion is proportional to the motive force impressed; and is made in the direction of the . . . [straight] line in which that force is impressed.
3) To every action there is always opposed an equal reaction."

exchange they gain protection for themselves and their property.

A government cannot, however, monitor or take away basic inalienable—or unchallengeable—natural rights. Locke insisted these are every human being's birthright. If and when a government no longer respects these rights, people have the right to overthrow the government and form a new one.

Locke also believed a human being is "naturally free, and nothing [should be] . . . able to put him into subjection to any earthly power without his consent."[8] Therefore, government can receive its authority from one source only—the people who are to be governed. Representatives elected by the citizens of a community should be the ones to engage in productive discussions that shape the final decisions that affect the community.

In addition to thinking about government, Locke also helped to popularize a new type of reasoning that became one of the intellectual currents of the Enlightenment.

Empiricism and a New Type of Reason

Because of the exciting advancements made during the Scientific Revolution during the seventeenth century, many thinkers were excited about the possibilities of human reasoning power. During this period, one of the most respected advocates of reason was French scientist and philosopher René Descartes. Like many of his counterparts in Europe, Descartes used a mathematical kind of logic to seek the truth. "Of all the sciences known as yet,

Arithmetic and Geometry alone are free from any taint of falsity or uncertainty,"[9] he wrote.

Such a mathematical way of thinking led Descartes to rely on a traditional way of reasoning called deductive when pondering important issues. This meant he often based his arguments on assumptions he merely believed were self-evident. For instance, he argued that all things must have a cause; thus, because humans have a concept of God in their minds, God must have caused that idea.

But another school of thought emerged in the eighteenth century that paralleled, and at times contradicted, deductive reasoning. It was advanced by philosophers

René Descartes used the principles of mathematics to philosophize about human behavior. He used deductive reasoning to interpret ideas about God and morality.

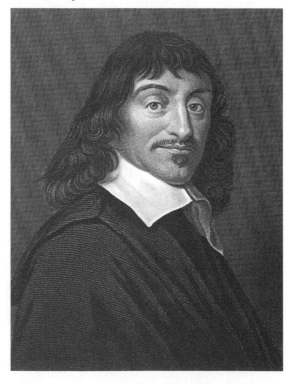

commonly called the British empiricists. These thinkers believed that Newton had demonstrated the importance of a new kind of reasoning, one based on empiricism; that is, information directly observed and experienced. Newton, insisted the empiricists, based his revolutionary concepts on observable facts, not just logic.

Locke, for example, stressed this point when he concluded that contrary to what other thinkers suggested, humans did not have any a priori, or preexisting, knowledge in their minds when they were born. There was also no divine revelation. That meant that humans were neither inherently good nor evil. Rather the mind was like a blank tablet, or tabula rasa. From birth, people gathered information from the outside world from the five senses. Everything humans knew came from experience.

Another British empiricist, George Berkeley, an Anglican bishop in Ireland, went even further than Locke. He argued that the human mind never actually perceives its environment at all. All it can really do is grasp its own mental perceptions of the outside world, not things themselves.

Scottish philosopher David Hume argued that the mind exists only as a tool that experiences momentary sensations and perceptions and nothing more. In his book *A Treatise of Human Nature*, published in 1739, he argues, "That which we call a *mind* is nothing but a heap or collection of different perceptions, united together by different relations."[10] All thinking, says Hume, whether sensations, reflections, or impressions, hinges on information introduced to the mind.

A common theme expressed by the British empiricists was that if experience alone created a sense of reality in the human mind, then it is the true measure of all things. This principle, they believed, could lead to a clearer understanding of human behavior. If people had minds filled with false impressions, superstitions, or wicked notions, the sources for such negative qualities must be bad environments and social institutions. By using reason based on observable fact to analyze social institutions and how to improve them, humans could greatly improve the conditions in which they lived.

The English Prelude to the Enlightenment

Amid the growing intellectual ferment caused by Newton, Locke, and other British thinkers, England underwent a radical shift in political power known as the Glorious Revolution. After unpopular Catholic monarch King James II fled England in 1668, the English Parliament crowned two Protestants, William and Mary, as their nation's new king and queen. Locke later wrote that since King James violated the rights of Englishmen, he deserved to be dethroned. The bloodless transition made when James, an absolute monarch, left the throne to Parliament taking on the role of appointing monarchs is why the revolution is deemed glorious.

Though England still had a monarchy, its lawmakers passed laws that restricted the powers of the king and queen. They also forbade monarchs to use the centuries-old claim that they had a God-given "divine right" to rule others. Parliament also passed a bill of rights for all English people

William and Mary are crowned by members of the House of Lords. England's bloodless transition from an absolute monarch to a government shared by Parliament and the monarchy was called the Glorious Revolution.

that granted equality before the law, the right to appeal to the government to redress grievances, the right to a speedy and fair trial, freedom from excessive fines and bail, and freedom from cruel and unusual punishments. Parliament made other lasting changes. It bestowed religious freedom to Protestants who were not members of the Church of England, and gave the English press greater freedom of expression.

England's Glorious Revolution had a profound impact on British political institutions. But it did little to improve or change many social and economic problems that persisted. Nonetheless, no European nation had ever guaranteed its citizens so many liberties. Europeans everywhere were astonished by what had occurred in England. Quite suddenly, this political revolution, combined with the ideas of its leading thinkers, thrust En-

gland forward as the cultural center of Europe. Thoughtful and creative minds across the continent now looked to the British Isles for inspiration. French philosopher Baron de Montesquieu observed of England, "It is the freest country in the world. I make exception of no republic and I call it free because the sovereign, whose authority is controlled and limited, is unable to inflict any imaginable harm on anyone."[11]

As the eighteenth century dawned, many more reformers in other European nations looked to England for guidance and inspiration.

Brewing Discontent

By now many areas of Europe were ripe for massive change. Unrest smoldered in almost every social class, especially among those at the lowest level. Serfdom, a political and economic system that imposed slavelike conditions on millions of Europeans during the Middle Ages, still persisted in Russia and other parts of eastern Europe. And although it had officially ended in Italy, England, the Netherlands, France, and areas of Germany and Spain, rural peasants in many of these nations still found themselves oppressed by ancient customs that obliged them to pay special taxes and render special duties to landowning nobles. Among French peasants resentment over these customs was intense.

Europe at the Beginning of the Enlightenment

Discontent was also evident in the social class above the peasants, the artisans, or skilled craftsmen. The centuries-old trade organizations to which artisans belonged had enormous economic power. In England they were called guilds. Similar organizations existed on the European continent and were known as compagnonnage. These organizations were commonly set up to benefit the workers of a town or village. They decided who could become a master craftsman. In addition, they set standards, prices, hours of employment, and working conditions and imposed restrictions on what kinds of products could be produced.

Since the Middle Ages, the guilds provided employment for young men and kept them out of mischief. They also discouraged poor workmanship and dishonesty. But by the eighteenth century, these organizations faced competition from a new class of businessmen who operated on a national, and even international level. These entrepreneurs raised enormous amounts of investment money, purchased raw materials, and arranged for products to be made cheaply by nonguild workers in their homes and cottages. The small tradition-bound guilds and compagnonnage experienced great difficulty in competing with these new large-scaled capitalistic undertakings.

Even Europe's rising middle class of merchants, bankers, and shopkeepers felt pangs of frustration. They resented the powerful nobles who held positions in the government and military and failed to live up to their responsibilities. Instead, corruption and incompetence were the rule, since many aristocrats spent their days living lives of luxury at the expense of the tax-paying lower classes.

Despite their advantages and privileges, many nobles were also dissatisfied with the status quo. They were envious of those who possessed even more power and status than themselves, Europe's absolute monarchs.

Europe's Absolute Monarchs

During the Middle Ages, political power was fragmented among numerous kings and warlords scattered across Europe. But by the eighteenth century a new trend toward consolidation of power into a single, all-powerful king was well under way. With the exception of Great Britain, most European nations were ruled by despotic monarchs who declared themselves imbued with divine right. Without rules to restrain them, most of these autocratic kings and queens felt themselves superior to all others, including nobles and clergy. These absolute monarchs ruled over all aspects of life within their boundaries. They taxed and spent public money as they pleased, censored free speech, and severely punished all critics.

As a result of unrestrained power in the hands of monarchs, judicial systems throughout Europe were all too often unjust, cruel, and irrational. Legal codes were generally a hodgepodge of contradictory rules rooted in the Middle Ages. Prisoners were routinely flogged, pilloried, tortured, beheaded, broken on the wheel, burned at the stake, and quartered. In Britain, the severed heads of traitors were publicly displayed. Many victims were often imprisoned indefinitely without ever being officially charged. Outside of England, bail was seldom set and jury trials rarely took place.

But Europe's absolute monarchs were not the only ones who possessed great power. Though its grip had weakened over the centuries, organized religion also wielded tremendous authority, especially the Catholic Church.

During the eighteenth century, traditional craftsmen such as these candlemakers faced stiff competition from large-scale manufacturers outside the established guilds.

During the Middle Ages, absolute monarchs were able to arbitrarily assess punishments for crimes, including burning at the stake. Such unfair treatment began to enrage the citizenry.

The Heavy Hand of Organized Religion

In England, religion was overshadowed by government. The Church of England, in fact, was controlled by the state. But on the European continent the situation was much different. Here, the Catholic Church was second in power and wealth only to the king and his army. A rich and bureaucratic institution that spread across Europe, the church exerted great influence over the lives of millions. It had the authority to exact a tithe, or tenth of the annual income of most Frenchmen. In some countries, it exclusively operated all public schools and universities. Though the church provided a needed service to the public, it also enjoyed a monopoly to propagate its own religious dogma. Church officials also had the power to censor any books, plays, and poems that displeased them. Any authors who expressed doctrines contrary to those of the church could be imprisoned and their works confiscated and destroyed.

The deeply rooted powers of the church and Crown were often intertwined and depended on and supported each other. In France, for example, the king received his authority from the church in the form of anointment and coronation. But he appointed all bishops within the church. And in some areas of the country, bishops picked all local judges and other government officials. Monarchs often expected—and received—public approval from the church for their actions. In return, church officials obtained special favors from royalty in the form of exemption from certain taxes or easy access to good government jobs for their friends and family members.

Deplorable Conditions

For the millions of Europeans who were neither nobles nor church officials, however, life was miserable. Farmers, laborers, and shepherds lived poverty stricken and disease ridden in isolated rustic villages. Thousands existed as serfs on estates owned by nobles and clergymen. In the cities, hordes of impoverished people led lives of despair and wretchedness in crowded, filthy, crime-ridden slums. Beggars and thieves wandered the streets.

Drunkenness abounded. Workers put in long hours and toiled in deplorable conditions. Child labor was common and life expectancy was low.

Despite breakthroughs in medical knowledge made possible by the Scientific Revolution, physicians did not yet understand how to cure, control, or prevent disease. The black plague, tuberculosis, polio, smallpox, diphtheria, cholera, and other diseases and maladies killed hundreds of thousands, especially young children. Mental illness was also badly understood. Few suspected that maladies of the mind might be caused by trauma, birth defects, or chemical imbalances. Instead, many Europeans believed the insane were possessed by demons. Some even clung to an old superstition that humans became "lunatics" by sleeping in the glow of moonlight.

A Philosophe's View of the Future

This portion of "Outlines of an Historical View of the Progress of the Human Mind," by French philosopher Marie Jean Antoine Nicolas Caritat, marquis de Condorcet, describes his vision of a future based on Enlightenment ideas. This excerpt appears in The Enlightenment, *edited by Frank E. Manuel.*

"Our hopes, as to the future condition of the human species, may be reduced to three points: the destruction of inequality between different nations, the progress of equality in one and the same nation: and lastly, the real improvement of [mankind].

Will not every nation one day arrive at the state of civilization attained by those people who are most enlightened, most free, most exempt from prejudices, as the French, for instance, and the Anglo-Americans? Will not slavery of countries subjected to kings, the barbarity of African tribes, and the ignorance of savages gradually vanish? Is there upon the face of the globe a single spot the inhabitants of which are condemned by nature never to enjoy liberty, never to exercise their reason?"

A wealthy landlord (right) surveys the living conditions of his impoverished serfs. In addition to poverty, serfs were often plagued by diseases resulting from malnutrition and unsanitary conditions.

The mentally ill and the demented were also a source of popular amusement. Special hospitals for the mentally ill, such as London's Little Bethlehem, or Bedlam, opened their doors to spectators who came to laugh and jeer at the wild behavior of deranged inmates.

Superstition was still rampant in the eighteenth century. Many Europeans believed in werewolves, fairies, ghosts, and demons. And though the practice was fading, many religious and government officials still accused women of witchcraft and burned them alive. Slavery existed in European overseas colonies.

Why was life so bleak for so many people? wondered a growing number of social critics. The obvious answer, they concluded, lay in the fact that their societies were badly structured and governed.

As the eighteenth century unfolded, criticism and protests against the status quo spread across Europe. But the voices that commanded the most attention—and gave vitality to the growing Enlightenment—came from France.

2 The Rise of the French Philosophes

France was the cultural hub of Europe during the eighteenth century. There the standards for philosophy, literature, fashions, manners, and a host of other human endeavors were set for Europeans—and Americans—everywhere. And it was there that the Enlightenment blossomed and commanded the attention of the world.

The troubling social problems all European states faced were especially intense in France. Here a complex, tangled web of social, political, and economic structures was known as the ancien régime. A concoction of ancient traditions and customs that bestowed power and privileges to a small minority, this corrupt system seemed to a rising tide of critics as a relic of the past.

For centuries, the French population had been grouped into three distinct social classes, or estates. The First Estate consisted of the clergy and the nobility comprised the Second. Though these two estates represented a mere 3 percent of the total French population, their members owned most of the land in France and held most of the important positions in the French government and military.

The other 97 percent of the population—merchants, city workers, and middle-class professionals, along with masses of peasants—made up France's Third Estate. This enormous population did most of the work and paid most of the taxes, which were all too often squandered by one French king after another.

Long-smoldering resentment over the abuses of the ancien régime came to a boil during the Enlightenment. In the early decades of the eighteenth century, French kings plunged their country into harmful and expensive wars. Many French people realized it was just a matter of time until crisis was upon them.

The Philosophes

During the early 1700s, a distinctive group of thinkers, writers, clergymen, nobles, and others emerged across France that zeroed in on the mounting societal problems of their day. In France, these dissidents were called philosophes. For the most part, they were not professional philosophers or university professors. Nor were they armed revolutionaries. Instead, they tended to be self-appointed social critics who believed their duty was to think critically and raise questions concerning the function of society. Rather than seeking power for themselves, most were content to shape public opinion on a wide range of topics they hoped would pressure government authorities to effect social changes. According to one Enlightenment philosophe:

> trampl[es] on prejudice, tradition, universal consent, authority, in a word all that enslaves most minds, [and] dares to think for himself, to go back and search for the clearest general principles, [and] to admit nothing except on the testimony of his experience and his reason.[12]

Most philosophes were accomplished writers. In a variety of literary styles they wrote and privately published an avalanche of books, articles, poems, plays, dialogues, pamphlets, and other works that launched the Enlightenment. Philosophes considered all of society's major institutions, such as its governmental, religious, and judicial systems, to be encrusted with prejudice, superstition, and corruption. However, they also believed this encrustation could be

The literary circle of Frederick the Great of Prussia engages in lively discussion. Frederick endorsed Enlightenment thinking for those of his own class.

scraped away by the power of reason and the scientific method. Immanuel Kant summed up the attitude of most philosophes: "Have courage to use your own reason!—That is the motto of the Enlightenment."[13]

They ridiculed superstition, ignorance, vanity, and fraudulent beliefs wherever they found them. Above all others, however, the main target of the French philosophe was the ancien régime—the monarchy, the nobles, and the established church. Philosophes saw this ancient order as an unjust system of inherited power, wealth, and status. They believed it selfishly created laws and traditions that be-

A Profile of the Philosophe

In this section from Henry Steele Commager's The Empire of Reason, *Denis Diderot explains his definition of a philosophe.*

"The Philosophe is a clock which, so to speak, sometimes winds itself.

A Philosophe, even in moments of passion, acts only after reflection; he walks through the night but is preceded by a torch.

Your Philosophe does not think he lives in exile in this world. He does not believe himself to be in enemy territory. He is an *honnete homme* [honest man] . . . who wishes to render himself useful.

The temperament of the Philosophe is to act out of a feeling for Order and Reason. . . . He is kneaded, so to speak, with the leaven of rule and of order. . . . He is suffused with concern for the good of the civil society, and he understands its principles better than other men.

Wickedness is as alien to the idea of a Philsophe, as is stupidity, and all experience shows us that the more rational and enlightened a man is, the more suited he is for the business of life."

Denis Diderot was the organizer and main author of the twenty-eight-volume Encyclopedia, *which was a compendium of Enlightenment ideas.*

The captain of a slave ship examines his cargo. Enlightenment philosophes protested slavery, which they believed was barbaric.

stowed riches, privilege, and power to royal families, nobles, and church officials at the expense of all others in society. And the philosophes yearned to replace this corrupt system with a new one that rewarded individuals who possessed natural talent and ability.

The philosophes often disagreed—sometimes vehemently—over the causes and solutions of the massive social problems that confronted them. Despite their differences, however, they shared many important basic beliefs. Among them were the principles emphasized by John Locke and other philosophers: free and open debate, religious tolerance, jury trials, and legal protection of individual rights.

Though philosophes were skeptical and critical in their writings, they were also optimistic. Most believed they lived in an exciting era of great potential for humanity. They expected important changes to take place in society as men and women learned to address their problems in a rational manner.

Most philosophes had faith in the human capacity for goodness. And this belief gave rise to a new humanitarian spirit that became a characteristic feature of the Enlightenment. Though many of their attacks on the ancien régime were cruel and unfair, most philosophes also expressed a genuine sympathy for humanity and called out for measures that would relieve suffering and wipe out injustice. They lashed out against the widespread use of torture and barbarous methods of execution commonly used by judicial officials. They also protested slavery, which still existed in many European nations and their colonies around the world.

The spirit of humanitarianism also convinced many philosophes that all humans should treat one another as brothers and sisters, no matter where they lived. Thus, many philosophes condemned war, which they believed was all too often waged for the benefit of greedy, power-seeking monarchs or fanatical clergymen. Some Enlightenment writers objected to nationalism within their own borders. In Germany, Kant even produced plans to promote international cooperation among nations.

Skepticism became a fashion, as the philosophes unleashed their criticism of eighteenth-century Europe. But they had only popularized this sort of intellectual approach; seventeenth-century thinkers had paved the way. Among them was the pioneer of the Enlightenment in France, Pierre Bayle.

The Father of the Enlightenment

Later known as "the Father of the Enlightenment,"[14] Pierre Bayle was born in 1647 in the village of Carlat near the French Pyrenees. At various times both a Catholic and a Protestant, Bayle became a university professor of philosophy at Rotterdam in the Netherlands. He first drew public attention in 1682 when he produced a pamphlet that discussed a great comet that appeared two years earlier and frightened the populations of Europe. Based on his knowledge of the latest research in astronomy, Bayle assured his readers that the comet was a scientifically predictable occurrence, not a supernatural omen as many believed.

During that same year, he also started a new magazine called the *News of the Republic of Letters* that brought him interna-

Pierre Bayle, often called "the Father of the Enlightenment" for his various projects and theories. Bayle's publications tried to inform the public about literature, science, philosophy, and other topics.

tional recognition. Bayle intended his publication to inform readers of the latest advancements in literature, science, philosophy, exploration, and other topics.

Not long afterward, he received shocking news: In France, the government and the Catholic Church organized a widespread campaign to persecute Protestants, known as Huguenots, and drive them out of the country. In the process, Catholics killed four members of Bayle's own family. Grief stricken and angry, he responded to all religious fanatics with a literary work entitled *Philosophical Commentary on These Words of Jesus Christ: "Compel Them to Come In."* He reminded his readers of a biblical parable told by Christ, "Go out quickly into the streets and lanes of the city, and bring in hither the poor, and the maimed . . . and the blind. . . . Compel them to come in, that my house may be filled." [15]

Bayle also urged religious tolerance for Muslims, Jews, and nonbelievers, an unpopular idea at the time. He condemned religious persecution of all kinds, including all the senseless bloodshed between Catholics and Protestants that had taken so many European lives.

The *Dictionary*

Although Bayle himself was a Protestant, some Dutch religious leaders vehemently attacked him for expressing skeptical ideas concerning faith. Eventually, he lost his position at the university, but this departure gave him time to work on his mammoth two-volume work, *Historical and Critical Dictionary*. "So, he remained quietly in his room, working fourteen hours a day, adding page after page to the strange volumes that were to become the fountainhead of the Enlightenment," [16] write historians Will and Ariel Durant.

Finally, the work was finished in 1697. Despite its title, the *Dictionary* was not a compendium of definitions. Instead, it mainly consisted of a variety of writings that expressed Bayle's version of history, literature, politics, philosophy, religion, and a wide range of other topics. Realizing his published words were likely to provoke many powerful authorities, Bayle cried, "The die is cast!" [17] as the book was being prepared for publication.

Among other things, Bayle attacked superstition and questionable beliefs in their many forms, including miracles and other extraordinary claims expressed in the Bible. He expressed doubt, for instance, that the biblical Eve really lived to the age of 940. Bayle also wondered how an all-knowing God could have created Adam and Eve and not known that one day they would sin and lose favor with him. How, he asked, could a god of goodness and perfection "produce a criminal creature? Can perfect goodness produce an unhappy creature?" [18]

Bayle's definition of evil also differed from that held by many theologians. "Every action committed against the light of conscience is essentially evil," [19] he wrote.

He was also skeptical of humanity. In his view, humans learned nothing from history and were doomed to repeat the mistakes of the past. Because human nature never changes, all their crimes and shortcomings are bound to happen again and again. That is why, Bayle argued, powerful governments were needed to keep social control.

As Bayle expected, the *Dictionary* was resented and publicly denounced. His own church congregation demanded that he appear before them to answer charges that he had used indecent expressions and espoused atheism.

Such actions, however, did nothing to stop the spreading influence and popularity of his two-volume work. His books remained immensely popular across Europe well into the eighteenth century. At least nine editions in several languages appeared. One admirer later called the first volume "the bible of the eighteenth century." [20]

Philosophers, thinkers, and writers everywhere admitted to being intellectually stimulated by Bayle's writings. "But of course the greatest influence of Bayle was on the *philosophes* of the Enlightenment [who followed Bayle]; they were . . . [nursed] on the Dictionnaire,"[21] the Durants point out.

One of these philosophes made it his personal duty to carry on the tradition of skepticism into the eighteenth century; he was a Parisian named François-Marie Arouet, better known as Voltaire.

Voltaire

Playwright, novelist, essayist, historian, philosopher, the multitalented Voltaire was one of the most astute critics of his age. In fact, suggests historian Sir Harold Nicolson, "The Supreme intellectual . . . influence of the eighteenth century was that exercised by Voltaire."[22]

But vanity and his razor-sharp wit often caused him trouble. His criticism of French authorities twice landed him in the infamous Bastille prison. On one occasion, Voltaire was severely beaten by the servants of a noble he had ridiculed.

At last in 1726 he was banished to England for three years. Ironically, his exile later proved perilous to the very people in France who exiled him. For while he was in England, Voltaire became enamored with the writings of Locke, Newton, and other English intellectuals. He also admired the government reforms the English had developed.

In 1729 he returned to his native land a fiery advocate of personal liberty and freedom of the press. Armed with these new ideas, he produced *Letters on the English Nation* in 1734. In this book, he explained the ideas of Newton and Locke to his fellow French citizens. He also fiercely attacked the ancien régime and celebrated the new political reforms of his beloved English.

Using words as weapons, Voltaire launched a lifelong attack against any practices that he believed violated basic standards of human fairness and decency. "To hold a pen is to be at war,"[23] he once declared. He opposed cruel treatment of prisoners and the indifference of the powerful to the weak and poor. He especially despised the iron grip the Catholic Church and the nobles held on society. Like many philosophes, he believed humans were by nature good. It was organized religion, he maintained, that corrupted them. Though he himself was a believer in God, Voltaire incessantly mocked church teachings of miracles and divine revelations.

Voltaire was a multitalented writer with a knack for cutting sarcasm and wit. His quote "to hold a pen is to be at war" succinctly expresses his philosophy toward his own writings.

Voltaire is arrested in France. Voltaire was so feared by the French monarchy that he was twice arrested and finally banned from Paris.

Voltaire's literary efforts earned him a reputation as a literary figure. But his mocking, sarcastic, and often insulting style also created many enemies. In 1758 the French government was so incensed with his ceaseless attacks that it banned him from Paris.

But his enemies failed to silence him. Fearful of reprisals, Voltaire moved to Ferney, Switzerland, not far from the French border. Here on a large estate he continued his virulent criticism of the ancien régime for twenty years, producing an astonishing output of words in many plays, essays, articles, letters, and novels. Over his lifetime, his personal correspondence numbered ten thousand letters. "About fif-

teen million of Voltaire's written words have come down to us, enough to make twenty Bibles,"[24] estimates biographer Theodore Besterman.

In these works, Voltaire attacked irrational and unjust laws and customs and ridiculed pompous and foolish religious and government officials who clung to archaic privileges. "Whatever you do, crush this infamy!"[25] he once thundered. By this, he meant the destruction of prejudice, superstition, ignorance, intolerance, creeds, and all other enemies of freedom.

Both widely praised by admirers and condemned by his enemies, Voltaire was indisputably the most influential individual thinker and writer of the eighteenth century. By his death in 1778, even monarchs such as Prussia's Frederick the Great, Catherine II of Russia, and Sweden's Gustavus III openly commended his work. He also became very popular among hard-pressed French commoners who considered him a revolutionary. The only intellectual force that rivaled Voltaire's influence was a controversial set of books that many Europeans wanted to burn.

The *Encyclopedia*

What began as a routine translation of an English encyclopedia for a French-language edition soon evolved into something much different. Under the supervision of a French translator and philosophe, Denis Diderot, a twenty-eight-volume encyclopedia eventually took shape that was unlike any previous undertaking. Working with French mathematician Jean Le Rond d'Alembert, Diderot published the set of books, one volume at a time, between 1750 and 1772.

The *Encyclopedia* was not merely a compendium of facts and definitions. It was also a forum for 140 of France's greatest as well as lesser-known philosophes who expressed the most current and enlightened views about almost every conceivable subject. Here they vented their criticism of societies, explored new ideas, and disseminated knowledge to the public. All major philosophical ideas, however, were subjected to a "naturalistic" or scientific analysis. Running throughout the work was a common thread: Reason, not tradition and religious expression, was the key to understanding and human progress. As Diderot explained:

Denis Diderot's Encyclopedia *drew criticism for its antireligious bias. Despite its critics, the* Encyclopedia *endured, giving philosophes a work that clarified and defined their ideas.*

All things must be examined, all must be winnowed and sifted. Without exception and without sparing anyone's sensibilities. . . . We must trample mercilessly upon all . . . ancient [juvenile ideas] . . . , overturn the barriers that reason never erected, give back to the arts and sciences the liberty that is so precious to them."[26]

Diderot wanted his project to spread the light of understanding over all human experience. He also desired to examine the meaning of concepts such as rights, authority, government, freedom, equality, and a host of other philosophical ideas.

But the *Encyclopedia* quickly became a source of controversy. For one thing, Diderot and his colleagues faced charges of plagiarism and inaccuracy. Guillaume François Berthier, editor of the Catholic

Goethe Praises the Philosophes

In these portions of personal letters that appear in Ariel and Will Durant's The Age of Voltaire, *Germany's Johann Wolfgang von Goethe expresses his indebtedness to the philosophes.*

"You have no idea of the influence which Voltaire and his great contemporaries had in my youth, and how they governed the [mind of the] whole civilized world. . . . It seems to me quite extraordinary to see what men the French had in their literature in the last century. I am astonished when I merely look at it. It was the metamorphosis of a hundred-year-old literature, which had been growing ever since Louis XIV, and now stood in full flower."

Johann Wolfgang von Goethe is well known for his play Faust, *which articulates many Enlightenment ideas.*

publication *Journal de Trevoux*, discovered over one hundred passages borrowed from other sources in the first volume of the *Encyclopedia* alone. In addition, many government and church leaders denounced the work as a thinly veiled attack against the monarchy and Catholicism. They repeatedly tried either to censor parts of the *Encyclopedia* or to stop its publication. King Louis XIV of France became so agitated at one point that he ordered the project halted after publication of the seventeenth volume.

Despite the actions of his enemies, Diderot managed to print the rest of the books in secrecy and deliver them to the thousands of subscribers whose patronage made the *Encyclopedia* possible. Outside of France, the book was also popular. The multivolume work was reprinted again and again. Pirated copies were made to keep up with demand. Across Europe, educated people looked on the *Encyclopedia* as a continuous source of information and inspiration that helped them understand similar problems in their own countries.

With its antireligious bias and its emphasis on science, technology, and philosophy, the *Encyclopedia*, more than any other published project, helped set the

The French encyclopedists are hard at work at Diderot's home.

Everything Has Been Discussed

In an essay that appears in Henry Steele Commager's The Empire of Reason, *Jean Le Rond d'Alembert, the coeditor of the* Encyclopedia, *states this proud view of the eighteenth century.*

"Our century has called itself the philosophic century par excellence . . . from the principles of the profane sciences to the foundations of revelation, from metaphysics to questions of taste, from music to morals, from the scholastic disputes of theologians to commercial affairs, from the rights of princes to those of people, from the natural law to the arbitrary laws of nations, in a word from the questions that affect us most to those that interest us least, everything has been discussed, analyzed, and disputed."

tone and clarify the issues of the Enlightenment. It also unified philosophes and their counterparts in Europe and gave them a sense of group identity. "Their solidarity lay in their awareness of a common foe—the *status quo*, and those who supported it, particularly Christianity and the Church,"[27] writes historian Lester Crocker.

Against this foe philosophes raised their pens to wage war. Their number-one opponent was the Catholic Church.

3 The Attack on Christianity

Nothing was more important to the philosophes than religious reform. They viewed the church as the main barrier to any solution to societal problems. Though the French philosophes were skeptical of all religions, they focused their attacks on the Catholic Church in France which they knew best. Their attacks, however, often extended to Catholic Church activities elsewhere in Europe.

Since many philosophes were either physicians or had a great interest in medicine, they tended to view organized religion as a major obstacle to the good health of European society. Some even viewed their campaign against Christianity as a battle against a social illness. As historian Peter Gay explains:

> Christianity, they wrote, was an infection, a "sacred contagion," a "sick man's dream," a germ sometimes dormant but always dangerous, always a potential source of an epidemic of fanaticism and persecution.[28]

A Profusion of Complaints

Obsessed with the idea that pure reason and science led to the discovery of truth, philosophes launched a widespread attack on the church to cure their society of the malady of organized religion.

As philosophes saw it, the church did great harm to society through many of its teachings. "The practices of existing church establishments were attacked as both unnatural and wicked, unnatural because they taught false doctrine and propagated a belief in the innate sinfulness of man, wicked because they bred cruelty and perpetuated superstition,"[29] explains historian Frank E. Manuel.

Philosophes hotly rejected the Christian doctrine of original sin, which held that humans were born into a state of sinfulness as a result of the fall of the biblical Adam and Eve. Only the grace of God, said the church, could redeem their souls.

But philosophes thought otherwise. As historian Louis Bredvold writes, "The revolutionary philosophers were all in agreement on the proposition that man is naturally good and that all the evil we are suffering is due to bad institutions and conventions."[30]

Another church teaching that rankled many philosophes was that of the so-called great chain of being. According to this idea, the various forms of life in the universe were laid out in a wide scale of descending order of importance. God stood at the top of this ladder of life. Then came angels, followed by monarchs, aristocrats, and so forth down to the lower social levels of human existence, beasts, and other forms of life.

Supporters of this concept believed it explained how God intended nature to be. Alexander Pope praises the idea in his "Essay on Man," published in 1732:

> Vast Chain of Being! which from God began,
>
> Natures ethereal, human, angel, man,
>
> Beast, bird, fish, insect, what no eye can see,
>
> No glass can reach! from Infinite to thee,

From thee to nothing.—Oh superior powers

. . . . .

> From Nature's chain whatever link you strike,
>
> Tenth or ten thousandth, breaks the chain alike.[31]

But critics attacked this notion. They held the chain of being was an unproved idea propagated by the members of the ancien régime to justify their position of privilege and to keep the poor and the oppressed fixed in their lowly places.

Philosophes also rejected the church's claim that religious conviction should be

A minister preaches to his congregation. The church was a favorite target of philosophes, who disagreed with Christianity's teachings of original sin and the great chain of being.

based on an unquestioning trust that whatever the church said was true, even if it contradicted everyday experience. Faith, asserted the clergy, was all that was necessary to support a belief in miracles, divine revelations, and other supernatural claims.

That was not good enough for most philosophes. These skeptics—especially those who had studied Newton, Locke, and other British philosophers—demanded that all religious claims be held up to a strict scrutiny based on reason and empiricism.

American statesman Thomas Jefferson made this very point in a letter to his nephew in 1785: "Fix reason firmly in her seat, and call on her tribunal for every fact, every opinion. Question with boldness even the existence of a God, because, if there be one, he must more approve of the homage of reason than that of blind faith."[32]

Religious skeptics raised many disturbing questions. Did Moses really part the Red Sea? Was it true that Christ rose from the dead? Was there really any solid evidence that the Bible was the Word of God?

This skepticism was joined by new insights about foreign religious and ethical systems other than Christianity. The Chinese, for instance, led orderly and ethical lives without the benefit of Christianity. In India, Hinduism provided a spiritual and ethical system for hundreds of millions of people. So too had Islam for many people in the Middle East, Africa, and beyond. The success of these religions flatly contradicted the Christian Church's assertion that only Christianity could serve as a spiritual and moral foundation for a society.

Philosophes found they were not alone in their opposition to the church. Others in France also detested the Catholic Church for its long tradition of intolerance, tax evasion, control of public education, and widespread persecution, torture, and killing of nonbelievers. The marquis d'Argension wrote in 1753 that

> it would be a mistake to attribute the loss of religion in France to English philosophy, which has not gained more than a hundred *philosophes* or so in Paris, instead of setting it down to the hatred against the priests, which goes to the very last extreme.[33]

Many French men and women were dismayed at the huge gulf that existed between poverty-stricken priests and their superiors, the bishops, who were often recruited from the nobility and lived in lux-

Thomas Jefferson was among the Enlightenment thinkers who believed that even concepts about God and religion should be put to the test of pure reason.

Bishops pose in their elaborate and expensive robes. Part of the people's resentment of the church came from the huge gap between the wealth of church officials and the poverty of their parishioners.

ury in the royal court. Some bishops had yearly incomes equivalent to hundreds of thousands of dollars. The archbishop of Strasbourg received over a million livre annually. (In 1750 one livre was roughly equal to about $6.32 in 1997.)

Critics believed such extravagance drained too much money and land away from the common people. The church paid no taxes on the enormous amount of land it owned. Like the aristocracy, it also kept thousands of French people working in near-bondage as serfs on its vast holdings. In addition, the clergy often used its authority to put pressure on Christians to bequeath their lands and fortunes to the church when they died. All these practices, according to the philosophes, propped up the ancien régime and kept the French populace trapped in ignorance and fear.

Politics too played a role. In France, many nobles quietly welcomed the philosophes' assault. These aristocrats had long resented the church's support of autocratic monarchs who they believed usurped much of their own power. At the same time, many middle-class merchants were also pleased with the philosophes. They believed their own social status would rise if the antireligion crusade caused church officials to lose authority and power.

Finally, philosophes disliked the idea that French Catholics were supposed to render their allegiance to a foreign power, i.e., the Vatican, the spiritual headquarters of the Catholic Church in Rome.

Differing Views of the Philosophes

Since philosophes differed in their own religious views, their criticism took many forms. Fearful of reprisals from church officials, some were cautious in their writings and avoided mentioning Christianity or the church entirely; instead, they made their arguments with references to non-specific organized religions. A few philosophes were bolder and more aggressive. Some wanted to merely reform the church; others, such as the philosophe Julien Offroy de La Mettrie, wanted to annihilate it: "Let us destroy the belief in God, the soul, immorality, and all Church dogma."[34]

For some religious skeptics, attacking Christianity became a form of entertainment. French aristocrat Seigneur de Saint Evremond, for example, enjoyed ridiculing Christianity for the amusement of dinner guests. However, he and other like-minded individuals did not put their satire in writing, since blasphemy was against the law. Instead, they memorized and recited their poems at private gatherings.

Not all expressions of religious doubt came from outside the church. Some emerged within the church community itself. As early as the Middle Ages, a group of Catholic scholars called the Scholastics attempted to use reason to develop logical arguments to support many of Christianity's claims. But whenever reason failed, these theologians fell back on faith and the counsel of St. Thomas Aquinas, a well-known Scholastic: "We attribute to Him things known by divine revelation, to which natural reason cannot reach."[35]

Nonetheless, the use of reason pioneered by Scholastics paved the way for the skeptical theologians of the eighteenth century. But many of these scholars took their inquiries further than their predecessors had; they questioned the truth of the very religion they were expected to defend. In fact, some of them even joined the philosophes in a new religious movement called Deism.

Deism

In 1624, in an essay on truth, *De veritate*, England's Lord Herbert of Cherbury became the first person to express the ideas that later developed into the belief system known as Deism. According to Herbert, human beings could not rely on the Bible to know religious truth. Instead, they should turn to several basic God-given ideas that were inborn in the minds of all human beings. These included a belief in a supreme being, the need for religious worship, virtuous living, repentance of wrongdoings, and the existence of a system of rewards and punishments after death. All major religions of the world contained nuggets of these basic truths, Herbert argued.

In time, admirers of his work formed a semireligious movement known as Deism, or God-ism. However, it was not a religion in the conventional sense of the word. Instead, it was a so-called natural religion based on natural law. Followers were a community of thinkers, not a congregation of believers.

Deists did not worship in Deist temples or churches. Nor did they sing special Deist hymns, pray, or listen to sermons. But most did believe in God. Their concept of God, however, differed from the personal God worshiped by most Christians. Instead, most Deists saw God as an impersonal supreme being who created a universe that operated according to divinely crafted natural laws. They were convinced that some sort of creator, or Grand Architect, had to exist to account for the

Playwright and philosopher Voltaire was a Deist who believed in a supreme creator.

presence of the vast, cosmic machinery of the universe. In Voltaire's famous analogy:

> When I see a watch whose hands mark the hours, I conclude that an intelligent being has arranged the springs of this machine, so that the hands mark the hours. Thus, when I see the springs of the human body, I conclude that an intelligent being has arranged these organs in order that they may be received and nourished nine months in the womb; that the eyes are given for seeing, the hands for grasping.[36]

Because Deism was not an organized religion with holy scripture and official doctrine, many varieties of the movement emerged. Some Christians were also Deists, but still believed that revelation from God and divine intervention into human lives was possible.

But other "philosophical" Deists dismissed all claims, such as miracles and divine revelation, because they appeared to violate natural law. They scoffed at biblical stories such as those of Adam and Eve and the resurrection of Jesus. These accounts, they said, were pure fiction. Prayers did not help either because God, a nonpersonal being who set the universe in motion, did not meddle with its machinery.

Deists also rejected the claim that Christianity held a monopoly on teaching virtue. They believed that universal moral laws could be found in the great cultures of the world, not just in Christianity.

Reason, of course, was the guiding principle of the religious critics. According to Deists, a religious understanding based on logic was far superior to accepting a belief system based on authority and threats imposed by the church.

A minority of philosophes went even further. They rejected not only religion, but God as well. In fact, they scolded Deists for compromising with priests and bishops. All religion is nonsense, argued these skeptics, because there is no God.

The Atheists

These nonbelievers, or atheists, were not satanists, or enemies of God. Rather, they were thinkers who were convinced that no supreme being existed. Some even doubted there had ever been a moment of creation. Why couldn't the universe always have existed? they asked. If so, there was no need to have a creator. Perhaps the universe is mere matter that obeys natural laws. All living things, including humans, are simply matter in motion. Such a materialist explanation of life boldly contradicted the Christian view that humans had souls that one day would be rewarded or punished by God.

In 1747 La Mettrie expounded on the materialist outlook in his book *L'Homme-machine (Man a Machine)*. He contended that a human being is a collection of biological parts that function like a well-tuned machine. La Mettrie rejected the idea that a soul or a mind could exist independently of the body. Instead, he said, the two are the same thing. Just look at the effect of a very high fever on a patient, he suggested. Delirium, a form of temporary madness, often results. This would not happen if the mind were truly a separate thing and immune from the effect of a bodily fever.

If humans were therefore only active matter with no spiritual connection to a creator, then La Mettrie saw no reason to worry about moral virtue. In other works, he exhorted humans to spend their lives living for the moment and seeking pleasure instead of trying to do the right thing to please God. Humans, he argued, were products of their surroundings and their heredity. What they did—even criminal acts—was a response to forces often beyond their personal control.

La Mettrie's works were widely read. They also provoked strong reaction. While some religious skeptics welcomed his insights, many Christians were incensed and vehemently criticized them. To escape arrest, he fled to the protection of one of his greatest admirers, the Prussian despot Frederick the Great.

German-born Paul-Henri-Dietrich d'Holbach, or Baron d'Holbach, another materialist, also commanded public attention with his ideas. Both a philosophe and an encyclopedist, he argued that there was no divine plan whatsoever: "Men have completely failed to see that this nature, lacking both good and evil intentions merely acts in accordance with necessary and immutable laws when it creates and destroys living things."[37]

He also believed it was a waste of time to wonder about the causes of the universe and whether there was a creator. Instead, he advised people to accept reality the way it appeared. And since this reality offered no proof of a divine helping hand, human beings were left alone in the universe to do the best they could.

Such a conclusion, however, did not convince d'Holbach to despair or to turn to wild living as recommended by La Mettrie. Although he was an atheist, the baron was also a highly principled individual who stressed the importance of morality in human affairs. Unlike theologians, he

Nothing but a Machine

This selection from Julien Offroy de La Mettrie's "Man a Machine," excerpted from Lester G. Crocker's The Age of Enlightenment, *reveals La Mettrie's conviction that the bodies and souls of human beings are biological mechanisms that respond in a machinelike manner to outside influences.*

"The human body is a machine which winds its own springs. It is the living image of perpetual movement. Nourishment keeps up the movements which fever excites. Without food, the soul pines away, goes mad, and dies exhausted. The soul is a taper whose light flares up the moment before it goes out. But nourish the body, pour into its veins life-giving juices and strong liquors, and then the soul grows strong like them, as if arming itself with a proud courage, and the soldier whom water would have made flee, grows bold and runs joyously to death to the sound of drums. Thus a hot drink sets into stormy movement the blood which cold water would have calmed.

To what excesses cruel hunger can bring us! We no longer regard even our own parents and children. We tear them to pieces eagerly and make horrible banquets of them; and in the fury with which we are carried away, the weakest is always the prey of the strongest."

believed moral living could be accomplished without the fear and superstition imposed by the church. He advocated acting in a virtuous way because such behavior contributes to a well-run, happy society that benefits everyone. As he pointed out in his book *A System of Nature,* published in 1770: "In a society guided by truth, experience, and reason, each man would know his true self-interest . . . and he would find real advantages or motives for doing his duties."[38]

D'Holbach's materialism shocked, enthralled, and entertained readers everywhere in Europe. But English empiricist David Hume took the skepticism of atheists one step further. He was skeptical of religion, philosophy, and even science itself. Trust nothing except what your senses tell you, he insisted. Even these sensations, he pointed out, were only impressions of reality, not reality itself. Therefore, humans can be absolutely sure of nothing.

The Church Strikes Back

Centuries of religious warfare and internal corruption had already traumatized Christianity. And by the eighteenth century, church officials watched in disbelief as the glare of the Enlightenment threatened to dissolve their authority and break the

Baron d'Holbach was a materialist who believed that the universe emanated from no divine plan and that it was pointless to speculate about the origins of the world.

backbone of Christian society. For obvious personal reasons, they resented the attacks. But along with many other Christians, they also considered the slurs and insults against Christianity as intolerable forms of blasphemy that had to be stopped.

So, a variety of "antiphilosophes" fought back. Across France, church officials attacked Deists, atheists, materialists, and any other philosophes who dared question church authority. According to the Durants, more than nine hundred written works appeared in defense of Christianity between 1715 and 1789. Church defenders published *La religion vengee,* a periodical

that delivered a monthly attack on the philosophes. In 1771 they also produced the *Encyclopedia methodisque,* an encyclopedia project that defended Christianity and was bigger than Diderot's.

The first line of defense for most religious writers and speakers was to assert church authority. The Catholic Church, they argued, was incapable of being wrong because it was God's holy institution. Furthermore, they pointed out, the moral authority of religion was needed to temper human behavior. Without a belief in a God who rewarded and punished souls in the afterlife, many people would feel free to

Reason Leads to Virtue

The Enlightenment, edited by Frank E. Manuel, contains this proposition made by Paul-Henri-Dietrich d'Holbach, also known as the Baron d'Holbach, who argues that reason, not religion, is what is needed for a virtuous life.

"To learn the true principles of morality, men have no need of theology, of revelation, or gods: They have need only of reason. They have only to enter into themselves, to reflect upon their own nature, consult their sensible interests, consider the object of society, and of the individuals, who compose it; and they will easily perceive that virtue is the interest, and vice the unhappiness of beings of their kind. Let us persuade men to be just, beneficent, moderate, sociable; not because the gods demand it, but because they must please men. Let us advise them to abstain from vice and crime not because they will be punished in the other world but because they will suffer for it in this."

Baron d'Holbach philosophized that morality was practical: If everyone obeyed society's rules, the world would be a more pleasurable place.

What Paine Believes

Often called the spokesman of the American Revolution, Thomas Paine was an avid proponent of the Enlightenment. The American Tradition in Literature, *published by W. W. Norton, contains this excerpt taken from Paine's pamphlet* The Age of Reason, *which clarifies the author's religious thinking.*

"I believe in one God, and no more; and I hope for happiness beyond this life.

I believe in the equality of man, and I believe that religious duties consist in doing justice, loving mercy, and endeavoring to make our fellow-creatures happy.

[However] . . . I do not believe in the creed professed by the Jewish church, by the Roman church, by the Greek church, by the Turkish church, by the Protestant church, nor by any church that I know of. My own mind is my own church.

All national institutions of churches—whether Jewish, Christian, or Turkish—appear to me no other than human inventions set up to terrify and enslave mankind and monopolize power and profit.

I do not mean by this declaration to condemn those who believe otherwise. They have the same right to their belief as I have to mine. But it is necessary to the happiness of man that he be mentally faithful to himself."

Enlightenment supporter Thomas Paine believed that only democracies can uphold humanity's natural rights.

do anything. Materialism, the antiphilosophes maintained, would lead to anarchy and savage behavior.

Some protectors of the church even employed reason to defend Christian faith. Bishop Joseph Butler of England, for instance, used a series of complex, logic-based arguments to assert that Deism did not satisfy the religious yearning within humans. Deism and other forms of natural religion advanced by philosophes, he said, were just as hard to believe as anything in the Bible.

Too much of the universe remained beyond the scope of reason. And that is why, according to Butler, people still needed faith.

But the church sometimes used harsher measures. Throughout the eighteenth century, many philosophes found themselves publicly accused of blasphemy and their works censored by the church. Some writers were imprisoned because their works offended powerful figures within the church hierarchy.

Most defenders of Christianity and the church made no apologies for their intolerance. They believed it was their duty to oppose any anti-Christian ideas that might lead Christians away from the true faith.

At times, they lashed out at philosophes and accused *them* of intolerance. Guillaume François Berthier, a leading defender of Christianity, wrote, "Unbelievers, you accuse us of a fanaticism which we do not have a semblance of possessing, while the hatred which animates you against our religion inspires in you a fanaticism whose too apparent excess are inconceivable." [39]

The Impact of Doubt

The intensity of the antiphilosophes' counterattack revealed how seriously the ancien régime considered the challenge of the Enlightenment. The skepticism of the philosophes, Deists, and atheists did make a powerful impact on many educated people not only in France, but also across Europe and America during the eighteenth century. But it did little to change the religious habits of most Christians. The offerings of Deism, materialism, and atheism proved to be too cold, barren, and purposeless for them. Many considered reason alone inadequate to satisfy the human yearning for meaning and purpose in life. There had to be something more, they believed.

By the middle of the eighteenth century, this dissatisfaction with reason had provoked a powerful widespread reaction that reshaped and redirected the Enlightenment.

4 Revolt Against Reason

By the mid–eighteenth century, a fresh wave of thinkers and writers surfaced in Europe whose views were at odds with older spokesmen of the Enlightenment. Though their goals were often the same as those of the earlier philosophes, these new social critics were disenchanted with reason. In fact, some of them argued that many of society's problems were caused by

Jean-Jacques Rousseau grew disenchanted with Enlightenment thinkers' emphasis on reason, preferring intuition, feeling, and emotion as guides to understanding the universe.

an overreliance on reason. As eighteenth-century French moralist Sebastian Chamfort put it, "In the present state of society, man seems to me to be more corrupted by his reason than his passions."[40]

And it was human passion that the new critics favored over reason. They praised human sentiment—emotion, intuition, feeling, compassion, and sympathy for other human beings, especially the downtrodden. These "sentimentalists" did not abandon the use of reason, but they were less likely to depend on logical thinking as a guide to truth. The human heart mattered more to them than the head.

Many influential thinkers and writers contributed to this revolt against reason, but the most powerful of them all—and perhaps the most influential philosophe of the Enlightenment—was a writer named Jean-Jacques Rousseau.

The Rise of Rousseau

Born in Switzerland, Rousseau spent much of his youth as a poor orphan. During this period, he acquired a love of nature and books and a hatred of injustice. These attitudes formed the foundations for his philosophical ideas.

Rousseau romanticized primitive people and societies, believing that because they lived closer to nature, their societies were better.

A drifter during his young adulthood, Rousseau garnered a variety of experience at different levels of European society. At various times, he was a young disciple in a religious community, a footman for nobles, a copier of sheet music, and a secretary for an ambassador in Venice. He was also a musician.

In 1745, Rousseau moved to Paris and fell into fashionable social circles where he met many well-known philosophes along with highly educated upper-class men and women who met regularly to discuss the latest ideas of the Enlightenment. But he soon discovered he did not share his new companions' passion for reason. By now he was highly skeptical of the emphasis philosophes placed on logic, rules, and structured systems. Instead, Rousseau favored intuition, feeling, and emotion. These natural feelings, he argued, rather than reason and book learning, would lead people in the right direction to live in the happiest way. "Reason deceives us only too often . . . but conscience never deceives,"[41] he once argued.

His first big chance to express his views to a large audience came in 1749 when, at age thirty-seven, he wrote a prize-winning essay in a contest sponsored by the Academy of Dijon. The topic: "Has the Progress of the Sciences and Arts Contributed to the Corruption or to the Improvement of Human Conduct?"

To Rousseau the answer was obvious: Humanity was indeed worse off. The advancement of knowledge without morality, he argued, not only gave government too much power, but it also corrupted people by filling their minds with unnatural desires. It had complicated their lives and robbed them of virtues, such as honesty and simplicity, that had graced human affairs in an earlier, more primitive time. "Let men learn for once that nature would have preserved them from science as a mother snatches a dangerous weapon from the hands of her child,"[42] he wrote. In a mad haste to become civilized, Rousseau concluded, humans had paid a tremendous price by surrendering their inclination to behave naturally.

Rousseau's words caused great controversy. Defenders of the scientific method were appalled. Voltaire heaped ridicule upon the new writer. But some members of the royal courts were pleased that someone had criticized the very ideals the philosophes stood for.

In addition to earning a gold medal and three hundred francs, Rousseau's essay made him famous and allowed him to explore his ideas further in other writing projects. In another essay, "Discourse on the Origin of Inequality Among Men," published in 1754, his bitterness toward the ancien régime was clear. He considered private property a great evil. Governments and laws were created, he wrote, to protect those who had acquired property at the expense of others. Even worse, slavery, serfdom, class divisions, and a host of other social problems resulted from the desire to own private property.

In this essay, Rousseau expounded on another favorite idea: Men and women were essentially good, but social institutions either corrupted or kept them from acting in a more natural way. He even suggested that primitive people in underdeveloped countries actually lived more happily than the modern French because they lived closer to nature and were not yet corrupted by civilized society. In closing, Rousseau invited readers to consult their hearts, ignore the voices of the status quo, and live a simpler, more natural life.

Rousseau expressed similar ideas in his novel *La Nouvelle Heloise,* published in 1761. A year later, in another novel, *Emile,* Rousseau argued that the educational system of eighteenth-century France filled the minds of young people with archaic ideas and prevented them from developing naturally into good, humane beings. Rousseau wrote, "When I desire to train the natural man, I do not want to make him a savage or to send him back to the woods: I want him to see with his own eyes and feel with his heart."[43]

"Everywhere in Chains"

Rousseau's most powerful work, *The Social Contract,* appeared in 1762. It opens with these stirring words, "Man is born free, but is everywhere in chains."[44] These chains, he argued, were the current social institutions that deprived humans of their natural freedoms. The way to break these restraints was to return to more natural relationships between humans that once existed before they were corrupted by society. Rousseau agreed with Locke that citizens had to give up their claims to absolute freedom in exchange for the greater benefits of community and the protection of a government.

An Evil Nature?

In this passage from Helvetius's De l'Homme (On Man), *which appears in* The Age of Enlightenment *edited by Lester G. Crocker, Helvetius refutes Rousseau's idea that humans are by nature innocent.*

"What does the spectacle of nature reveal to us? A multitude of beings destined to devour each other. Man especially, say the anatomists, has the teeth of a carnivorous animal. He must therefore be voracious, consequently cruel and bloodthirsty. Moreover, flesh is for him the most healthful food, the most fit for his structure. His self-preservation, like that of almost all animal species, depends on his destroying others. Men, scattered by nature across the vast forests, were hunters first. When they drew together and were forced to find nourishment within a smaller space, need made them shepherds. Still more numerous they finally became food growers. In all of these diverse situations man is the born destroyer of animals, either to nourish himself on their flesh, or to defend the cattle, fruits, grains, and legumes necessary to his survival against them."

But this voluntary surrender of freedom for a greater good, he said, was the only justification for government.

According to Rousseau, governments may vary: "Monarchy . . . is suited only to wealthy nations; aristocracy, to States moderate both in wealth and size; democracy, to small and poor States." [45]

However, any legitimate government, he stated, derives "its existence . . . from the . . . [social] contract . . . [and] . . . neither has nor can have any interest contrary to [that of the community]." [46]

Throughout *The Social Contract,* Rousseau expresses some of the most radical statements of his age. For instance, he again questions the property rights that allowed some people to possess enormous tracts of land: "Every man has by nature a right to all [land] that is necessary to him . . . [but once his] portion has been allotted, he ought to confine himself to it." [47]

Elsewhere he wonders: "If we ask in what precisely consists the greatest good of all, which should be the end of every system of legislation, we shall find it reduces itself to two main objects, liberty and equality." [48]

Though many of Rousseau's ideas seem confused, overly sentimental, and contradictory, the impact of much of his work was powerful and electric. Across Europe supporters of democracy, anarchism, and individual freedom drew inspiration from Rousseau's writings. In France, the common people—whom Rousseau often disdained—saw him as a champion and an opponent of the ancien régime. "No other

Rousseau enjoys the beauty of Switzerland. Ironically, while common people were inspired by Rousseau's attitudes toward equality and nobility, Rousseau despised commoners, believing them ignorant and superstitious.

secular book has shaken modern society more violently than the brief *Social Contract*,"[49] writes historian Arthur May.

Not everyone was as enthusiastic. Many philosophes, for example, saw his work as a step backward in the fight against irrationality. European monarchs were also displeased. They disliked his skepticism of divine right and his questioning of authority.

And when the French officials of the local governments of Geneva and Bern condemned his works, Rousseau had to flee first to Prussia and later to England for protection. Years later, when the furor caused by his book died down, he was allowed back into France. But for the rest of his life, he was haunted by fears of persecution.

A Wave of Sentimentality

Rousseau's works not only caused political controversy, but also popularized a wave of sentimentality that swept Europe in the second half of the eighteenth century. This widespread interest in human passion was not entirely a reaction against reason, however. Some Europeans considered the shift to sentimentality a natural progression of the Enlightenment. With their attack on authority and traditions, the earlier philosophes had unleashed powerful emotions and ideas of all sorts. They had awakened the human spirit and all its many moods and varieties. "In the late eighteenth century, sentimentality was part of a . . . process . . . by which civilization was being made more human and more humane,"[50] suggests scholar Peter Gay.

The preoccupation with human sentiment also arose from a sweeping dissatisfaction with those who championed the power of reason. Many Europeans thought the cold, impersonal scientific method advocated by philosophes had failed to improve society very much. In fact, the ancien régime seemed as securely entrenched as ever.

In addition, many Europeans were skeptical of the rational, well-organized society with well-defined principles and rules of behavior advocated by the philosophes. Some were appalled, for example, at the suggestions made by one reason-loving French government official who argued that the government ought not hold down food prices because such efforts went against the "natural order." Instead, he argued, prices should be allowed to rise to their natural level even if starvation resulted. Increased profits from these higher prices, the official said, would stimulate investment in future agricultural projects.

Such logic prompted Jacques Necker, a popular French financier, to reply: "I simply cannot understand this cold intellectual compassion for future generations, which is supposed to harden our hearts against the cries of the thousand unfortunates who surround us now."[51]

Champions of human sentiment also charged that a rigid society based solely on reason would stifle individuality and creativity. Many instead argued that if men and women relied on their emotions instead of their intellects, they would be more creative and more likely to solve the problems the philosophes had failed to conquer.

In fact, Rousseau and his supporters were convinced that emotion was superior to reason as a means of solving social and moral problems that plagued humanity. They believed the human heart was a direct path to the conscience, and the conscience was the best tool for making moral decisions.

Historian Louis Bredvold suggests that "a disposition to tears was not only a proof of a genuine moral sensibility; it was itself an exercise in virtue, a moral conditioning of the heart."[52]

Respect for Nature

Sentimentalists also celebrated the natural world. This interest was sparked in part by stories told by European explorers and scholars who ventured to faraway, exotic places. Europeans were enthralled by accounts of primitive people who reportedly lived happy, simple lives close to nature. Of special interest were tales of South Pacific islanders and the tribes of native North Americans. They were even enthralled by tales of colonial Americans. Americans, it was widely believed, lived closer to nature,

Emotional Control

Quoted in Norman Hampson's The Enlightenment, *philosophe Baron de Womar makes this observation about reason and human emotions.*

"Cold reason never produced anything distinguished and the only way to overcome one passion is by setting another against it. When the passion of virtue arises, it rules absolutely and holds all the rest in equilibrium. That is what makes the real sage, who is no more sheltered from the passions than anyone else, but who alone knows how to conquer them by themselves, as a pilot holds his course though the winds be contrary."

and thus more admirably, than their European counterparts. Many Europeans also had a special fascination with the American statesman Benjamin Franklin. His simple manner of speech and dress, along with his reputation as a writer, inventor, Deist, and political leader helped make him a hero across France. Franklin's popularity soared in 1776 when he arrived in Paris on a diplomatic mission seeking economic and military assistance from the French government. Huge adoring crowds surrounded him wherever he appeared in homespun clothes and a beaver skin hat, instead of the ornate embroidered silks and powdered wigs favored by fashionable Frenchmen of the day.

A preoccupation with "noble savages" and the desirability of living in harmony with nature became a fad in Europe. For recreation many wealthy people chose to socialize with their friends in the countryside or take long treks through the woods and mountains. Even France's queen, Marie-Antoinette, was so smitten with the idea of natural living that she pretended to be a simple shepherdess in the gardens of her palace outside Paris. Dressed in a straw hat and a modest white gown, she also made daily visits to a nearby park that she had converted into a village of eight small cottages that housed several families transported from the countryside. Here, she happily watched the villagers milk cows and perform other farming chores.

Many of the best-selling books of this period reflected the growing interest in nature. One of the most popular was the novel *Robinson Crusoe*, written by English writer Daniel Defoe. Appearing in 1719, it is the tale of a man marooned on an apparently uninhabited island. His eventual

Benjamin Franklin (with cane) is presented to the French court. Franklin's rough clothing and simple ways were greatly admired by the French, who called him "un homme natural."

In an attempt to return to the simple, rural lifestyle that Rousseau recommended, French queen Marie-Antoinette had a replica of a small village built to use as a retreat. Marie-Antoinette would often pretend she was a simple shepherdess in the elaborate surroundings.

companion is a savage named Friday. To survive, Crusoe must live by his own wits and obey the dictates of the natural world. He has to build his own home, sew his own clothes, bake bread, plant a garden, and construct a table and chairs—and even an umbrella—from materials salvaged from his shipwreck.

Passion was a common literary theme in the revolt against reason. Across Europe, readers turned to emotion-packed stories of distressed young women torn between passion and restraint, such as the novels *Pamela* and *Clarissa* by English author Samuel Richardson.

Sentiment and feeling were also important to Johann Wolfgang von Goethe, Germany's widely admired biographer, poet, playwright, novelist, translator, and natural scientist. Unlike many of his counterparts in France, Goethe dwelled on the emotional side of human life. His novel *The Sorrows of Young Werther* is a highly sen-

timental, depressing story of a lovesick young man who takes his own life. So powerfully engaging was the novel that many young men in Europe felt compelled to dress in sky-blue coats, yellow breeches, and jackboots just as Werther did. Some troubled readers carried their imitation too far when they joined their fictional hero in suicide.

As literature continued to reflect the growing public interest in human sentimentality, other forces were joining in the backlash against reason.

A Renewal of Religious Feeling

Across Europe many Christians were displeased with the emotional and spiritual dryness of mainstream religious faiths. Though Deism was never fully and openly

The hero in The Sorrows of Young Werther, *by Johann Wolfgang von Goethe (pictured), is so highly sensitive and emotional that he eventually takes his own life. The novel sparked many young men to wear clothing and take on attitudes that emulated Werther.*

embraced by many in Great Britain outside the educated upper classes, its influence was nonetheless widespread on mainstream religious thinking. To their dismay, religious leaders, pastors, and their congregations saw many of their traditions and central beliefs questioned, and even ridiculed, by Deist thinkers. Some of this criticism brought useful reforms, however. Many Christians, for instance, became more open-minded, less superstitious, and more tolerant as a result of the Deist influence.

But these changes came at a cost. Some believers felt their faith had been deprived of spiritual value. Church service for great numbers of English people had become a sterile, uninspiring ritual dominated by the Anglican Church, England's official religion. Many Christians found church life so bland and uninspiring that they abandoned religious service alto-

gether. Even as early as 1728, the French *philosophe* Montesquieu observed, "In England there is no religion and the subject, if mentioned in society, evokes nothing but laughter."[53]

Several religious movements emerged to fill this spiritual void. In England, brothers John and Charles Wesley, along with Charles Whitefield, launched a crusade in the 1740s to bring emotion, faith, and spirit back into church worship. They preached in a manner that was far different from that usually heard elsewhere in England. Instead of dry, intellectual sermons, these men offered emotionally charged worship services that emphasized faith over good works and the joy of God's forgiveness of sins. The Methodists, as followers of the Wesleys became known, soon took their message to rural populations who were especially receptive to an emotional approach to religion.

On the other hand, England's upper-class Christians—who physically segregated themselves from the lower classes during church services—were appalled by the public "emotionalism" of the lower classes and strove to distance themselves from it.

Another religious movement to restore emotion and spirituality to religion, called Pietism, appeared in Germany during the eighteenth century. Like Methodism, Pietism was originally a name bestowed as ridicule by critics. It emphasized repentance, faith, and direct communication with God without the help of a priest. Pietists stressed "the religion of the heart" rather than that of the intellect.

Pietism had special appeal to German Christians who were weary of the restrained rituals and unwavering attitudes

John Wesley preaches on his father's grave while admiring crowds seem to swoon with emotion and reverie. In his moving sermons, Wesley attempted to woo worshipers back to church.

of the Lutheran Church. Among them was Immanuel Kant, a German philosopher who attempted to fuse reason, the spirit of humanitarianism, and faith into a single system of thought.

Immanuel Kant

Kant was a gifted, deep-thinking, reserved professor who never ventured far from Königsberg, Germany, the university town where he lived and worked most of his long life.

Kant's mind, however, was very well traveled in the world of ideas. An enthusiast of the Enlightenment, or the Aufklärung, as it was called in Germany, Kant was also a religious person whose spirituality had been shaped in part by Pietism.

As a philosopher, he tried to forge a compromise between reason and the human heart. Like many European philosophers, he believed scientific inquiry could uncover the laws of nature and perhaps even help explain moral and ethical aspects of human life. But thanks to the writings of Rousseau, he also was skeptical of relying too heavily on reason.

Kant also agreed with David Hume's suggestion that what humans knew was based on whatever the five senses conveyed to the mind. But, as he pointed out in his philosophical masterwork *The Critique of Pure Reason,* published in 1781, something amazing happens when a flood of impressions rushes across the human mind. Somehow, the mind intuitively makes sense of the millions of random sensations that keep appearing. It sifts and sorts through them. It categorizes them. It forms ideas out of these otherwise random impressions.

How does all this take place? According to Kant, the blank tablet idea of Locke

An Antiphilosophe Strikes Back

Among those who opposed the philosophes was the scholar and religious conservative Elie Catherine Freron. In this passage excerpted from Ariel and Will Durant's The Age of Voltaire, *Freron chides the philosophes for upsetting the social order.*

"Never was there an age more fertile than ours in [disloyal . . . writers who . . . concentrate all their powers on attacking the Godhead. They call themselves apostles of humanity, never realizing that it ill befits a citizen, and does a grave disservice to mankind, to rob them of the only hopes which offer them some mitigation of their life's ills. They do not understand that they are upsetting the social order, inciting the poor against the rich, the weak against the strong, and putting arms into millions of hands hitherto restrained from violence by their moral and religious sense quite as much as by the law."

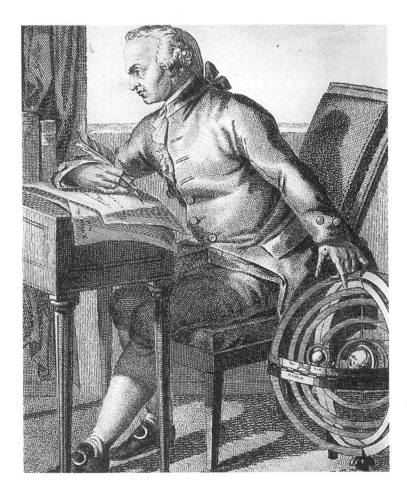

Immanuel Kant believed that humans had an innate sense of right and wrong. This moral sense, Kant argued, served as a reason to believe in God.

and others was not completely correct. Some preexisting ideas do exist. Human beings, Kant argued, have inherent qualities in their minds designed to give meaning to what would otherwise be a swamp of endless, unrelated impressions transmitted to the mind by the eyes, ears, tongue, nose, and fingers. Quantity, quality, and cause and effect are just some of the concepts that help to make sense of this rush of information. And these ideas existed in the mind at birth.

The use of reason can explain how many thoughts enter the human mind, as Locke suggested. But it cannot be used to prove concepts such as the existence of

free will, immortality, and the existence of God. These notions, Kant says, arrive in the human mind independently of the senses. Where do they come from? Kant does not say. But the fact that they do arrive, he says, implies that humans have, among other things, an inborn sense of right and wrong.

And this moral sense commands people to do the right thing when they are faced with an ethical problem. Kant believed everyone should act in a way that would serve as a universal rule for all others to follow. He also argued that they should never use anyone as a means to an end.

Kant concluded from his years of philosophical study that this inherent moral sense in human beings, and not reason, was the most compelling basis for religious belief, and it demanded that humans believe and act as if there was a God, if for no other reason than to give meaning to life and to control society.

Despite his fondness for difficult and long-winded prose, Kant's effort to blend the best of reason and sentiment successfully impressed many among the educated classes of Europe. But because he sought to find a compromise, or common ground between the two approaches, he managed to both insult and please many philosophes, religious leaders, and other thinkers. His ideas were so new and insightful that they became one of the sources for a new school of philosophy, called Idealism, that parted with the spirit of rationalism.

Kant's ideas also caused a major shift in philosophy and a turning point in the Enlightenment. One of the original concepts of the Enlightenment is that there are laws of nature that human beings can discover. According to Kant, "It is the other way around," writes philosophy professor T. Z. Lavine. "The mind gives its own laws to nature—its own laws in the form of its own necessary concepts which form, organize, and structure all our experience, all our knowledge of nature. In Kant's famous words, 'Mind is the law-giver to nature.'"[54]

Kant and all other skeptics of pure reason did not end the main thrust of the Enlightenment, but they did change it. During the second half of the eighteenth century, the Enlightenment became both "the Age of Reason" and "the Age of Feeling."

5 The Campaign to Reform Society

Fueled by both reason and sentiment, the Enlightenment became the most important intellectual force of the eighteenth century.

Although reducing the power and influence of organized religion was the philosophes' most important and urgent task, they also waged a vigorous campaign to reform many other institutions of society. Among their chief concerns was how to improve government, which most philosophes considered to be antiquated, unfair, and inefficient.

How to Have Enlightened Rule

As a rule, however, the attack against government, especially in France, was less unified than the one waged against the church. For one thing, many Europeans simply did not much care which type of government ruled over them. They merely wanted a government that worked well. Alexander Pope summed a common sentiment towards government:

> For forms of government let fool contest;
> Whate'er is best administer'd is best.[55]

Nonetheless, many of the leaders of the Enlightenment had strong political preferences. But the debate hinged on this: Should reform come from above or below? Many philosophes answered this question by voicing support for the continuation of monarchy. They, like many Europeans, agreed with seventeenth-century English philosopher Thomas Hobbes, who argued that human nature was essentially narrow-minded and self-centered. Only with strict laws and an all-powerful monarch could the cruelty and selfishness of humans be kept under control.

Voltaire supported this view, though he and other philosophes wanted "enlightened" monarchs. Such rulers, they believed, would be better than autocratic despots, the self-serving aristocrats who composed the French government and controlled much of society. But other social critics thought the main obstacles to good government were the monarchs themselves. Not only did these skeptics scoff at the idea of divine rule and hereditary rule, they also believed monarchy was a relic of a bygone era that had no place in the modern world. In their view, nothing less than the total abolition of all forms of monarchy would suffice. "And with the guts of the last priest let us strangle the last king!"[56] Diderot once wrote.

An Enlightened Despot Makes His Point

Frederick the Great, the despot of Prussia, considered himself an enlightened ruler. This passage, extracted from Wallbank, Taylor, and Carson's Civilization: Past and Present, *reveals the monarch's view of how a humane monarch ought to act.*

"Princes and monarchs . . . are not invested with supreme authority that they may, with impunity, riot in debauchery and voluptuousness. . . . The sovereign represents the States; he and his people form but one body, which can only be happy as far as united by concord. The prince is to the nation he governs what the head is to the man; it is his duty to see, think, and act for the whole community. . . . The monarchy is only the first servant of the State, who is obliged to act with [integrity] and prudence, and to remain as totally disinterested as if he were each moment liable to render an account of his administration to his fellow-citizens. . . . As the sovereign is properly the head of a family of citizens, the father of his people, he ought on all occasions to be the last refuge of the unfortunate."

Prussian king Frederick the Great considered himself an enlightened monarch.

What many of these more radical thinkers wanted instead was a form of government that many Europeans considered radical and dangerous, a system called democracy.

This idea too caused divisions of opinion. Few reformers advocated pure democracy, such as that practiced by the ancient Greeks. In this system, all citizens took part in making laws and governmental decisions.

Instead, most advocates of a democratic form of government preferred a republican form of government, such as the one created after the American Revolution, in which citizens elect representatives to pass their laws and policies.

Rousseau, however, thought even this was unwise. He favored the election of government administrators and judges, but not lawmakers. Once representatives got into office, he argued, they tended to pass laws to satisfy their own interest, not that of the community as a whole. Instead, he advocated the creation of laws by citizens themselves at a general assembly.

A handful of thinkers advanced an even more radical idea: communism. Under this system, all class distinctions would be abolished. All citizens would be equal in status and all phases of the economy and politics would be controlled by an all-powerful leadership.

In his "Laws for a Communist Society," an eighteenth-century Frenchman known only as Morelly wrote, "Nobody will own anything in the Society individually or as an estate, except the thing which he is currently using for his needs, his pleasures, or his daily work. Every Citizen will be a public person, supported, maintained, and employed at Public Expense."[57]

Though such ideas never gained favor during the eighteenth century, they did lay the groundwork for future thinkers whose works led to the creation of communist governments in Russia, China, and eastern Europe in the twentieth century.

All talk of democracy in any form infuriated many Europeans. Voltaire, for instance, opposed giving power of any sort to the common people, whom he viewed as a poor, malnourished, superstitious, and uneducated mass. "I do not like government by the rabble,"[58] he wrote. Others believed common folk were simply too corrupted by ignorance and superstition to make sound decisions.

Despite their differences, political reformers agreed that some sort of reform was needed. And one topic they agreed on was the need to limit the potential abuse of power.

The Need for a Balance of Power

Even fiery radicals such as those who led the American Revolution realized that all forms of government, even democracy, could prove to be as abusive and tyrannical as any absolute monarch. How could any government function without creating an absolute dictatorship? One solution to this problem emerged in the writings of French philosophe Charles de Secondat, baron de Montesquieu.

A member of the privileged class in France with close ties to the nation's powerful leaders, Montesquieu was considered

Baron de Montesquieu did not believe that society was governed by innate, natural laws. He believed in gathering facts and observations before undertaking any actions or adhering to any principles.

the first great political analyst of his age. Unlike many philosophes, he was skeptical of the idea of natural laws in human affairs. Like a scientist, he preferred facts. His advice was to observe and gather as many facts as possible that were crucial to any issue before undertaking any action. By following such a meticulous path, he reasoned, lawmakers could make informed judgments about how to govern.

Montesquieu concluded that many possible forms of government could work well. In his masterpiece, *The Spirit of Laws,* which appeared in 1748, he argued that a country's unique history and culture dictated the type of government it should have. Though Montesquieu believed no single government was best, he was nonetheless an ardent supporter of freedom and an opponent of all forms of tyranny. And like Voltaire, he was a great admirer of the English Parliament. What particularly commanded his respect was English measures to maintain a separation of power between three different branches of government. The king and his ministers were responsible for executive duties. This meant they carried out the laws and performed administrative responsibilities. Lawmaking was the task of members of Parliament, the second branch of government. Judges made up the third branch; their duty was to pass judgment on accused lawbreakers, settle legal disputes, and interpret laws.

Montesquieu believed this separation of powers was the key to successful government because it prevented the concentration of power in the hands of any single individual or group. "There is no liberty, if the power of judging be not separated from the legislative and executive powers,"[59] he wrote.

A session of the English Parliament. Many Enlightenment thinkers especially admired England's government because it took care to balance powers between three different branches of government.

Russian serfs plow the fields of the steppes. Philosophes criticized governments that maintained such great inequalities between the rich and the poor.

Though his favorable analysis of the British parliamentary system was somewhat inaccurate, it nonetheless influenced the creators of the U.S. Constitution in the late eighteenth century, which provides for a federal government operating under a system of divided powers similar to the one praised by Montesquieu.

Economic Reform

In their analysis of government, French philosophes and fellow European critics also criticized the influence of the political system on the economic health of a nation. They complained, for example, that serfdom still existed in Russia and many eastern European countries, where millions of rural people were forced to live on the lands where they were born and work for a lifetime in a condition of near-slavery for the benefit of a class of landowning nobles. Similar, though less severe, conditions affected the lives of millions of rural villagers in western Europe. In France, nobles still enjoyed centuries-old privileges

that granted them the right to exact duties and taxes from commoners who lived and worked on their lands.

Still other ancient customs and traditions shackled trade and commerce practices to the past. For instance, many sons of artisans were not free to pursue an occupation of their choosing. Instead, tradition, backed up by local laws, obliged them to follow the trade or occupation of their fathers. Guilds set rigid guidelines that regulated how products could be made and by whom.

Philosophes and social critics throughout Europe wanted to break with such practices. They insisted that people should have the freedom to choose their own occupations and live where they wanted. In addition, they argued for the right of commoners to buy land without the interference of nobles in the transaction, as was often the case.

Free Trade Issues

Some philosophes also took aim at mercantilism, the prevailing national economic policy in most western European nations. This policy required the government of each nation to regulate almost all aspects of its economy, i.e., its exports, imports, and its production and distribution of goods and services. Each mercantilist nation also assessed taxes on imported goods to protect domestic industries from competition abroad. These taxes also aided the nation's own exporting companies.

The main objective of mercantilism was to assure that a nation could sell more products to other countries than it bought. Supporters of this system believed such tight governmental control was needed to guarantee the nation's economic independence.

But these assumptions came under powerful attack from a group of French thinkers called physiocrats, led by François Quesnay, a royal physician. Physiocrats claimed mercantilism was inefficient and failed to create prosperity for all. Instead, they favored their own system of economics, which they claimed was based on natural law. According to their view, money flows through an economic system and obeys certain natural laws in the same way that blood does when it circulates through a living organism. An economy that was left alone by government to respond to these natural laws, they argued, would outperform mercantilism.

According to a popular story, French king Louis XV once asked Quesnay what he would decree if he were king. "Nothing," replied the physiocrat.

"Who, then, would govern?"

"The laws," Quesnay responded, referring to the natural laws of economics.[60]

In 1776, Adam Smith, a Scottish professor, carried the arguments of the physiocrats even further with the publication of

Adam Smith worked to define the natural laws that he said governed commerce. The first law, Smith argued, was the law of self-interest.

his book *An Inquiry into the Nature and Causes of the Wealth of Nations.* Among other topics, he clarified the "natural laws" that mercantilism ignored.

The Natural Laws of the Economy

The first of these laws was self-interest. According to Smith, people labor to benefit themselves, not others. But this seemingly selfish interest benefits the entire economy when the other two natural laws are allowed to function.

One of these is competition. In a free market not controlled by governments or guilds, producers are forced by competition to produce better goods and services and to sell at lower prices to stay in business.

The third natural law is supply and demand. What really causes someone to take the time to make a product and offer it for sale? The answer, Smith suggests, is the producer's desire to make a profit. But a producer can succeed only if there is a demand or a desire among consumers for that product.

According to Smith, this process of supply and demand is based on freedom in the marketplace. Producers are free to charge whatever prices they want, and consumers have the liberty to buy or reject those goods.

Smith implored governments to retreat from mercantilism. He disapproved of fixed wages, the rigid rules of guilds, and any government regulations that limited the economy. He also advocated free trade among nations and urged governments not to try to protect their domestic industries with overly high import taxes, nor hinder foreign competition. It was far better, he said, to allow natural law to determine what products are made and how much they are sold for, even at the international level. When nations and individuals are free of undue governmental restraints, Smith argued, they tend to live up to their capacity for achievement and create prosperity along the way.

A strong advocate of reason, Smith wrote that by analyzing "the political economy," a nation's decision makers could go far in advancing the prosperity of both the masses and their ruling classes.

But contrary to what some of his critics thought, Smith did not favor allowing businesses and industries to do absolutely anything they wanted, especially if they harmed poor working people. In fact, he was sympathetic to the working class and favored high wages during periods of business prosperity. A booming economy, he believed, should benefit the entire society, not just the rich and powerful.

The Wealth of Nations is a hefty, slow-paced book. Several years passed before its impact became widespread. Eventually, however, it became the bible of classic economics in Europe during the nineteenth and twentieth centuries.

Overhauling the Legal System

Another institution that commanded the philosophes' attention was the judicial system. In France, as elsewhere, laws were not always written down. In some places, tradition, superstition, and the privileged classes of the ancien régime determined a great number of rules by which people were expected to live. Generally, these laws were arbitrary, unfair, and cruel, especially when applied to the lower classes. Even small infractions, such as a perceived lack of respect shown during a religious ceremony, could earn a commoner imprisonment or torture. A noble, on the other hand, might escape punishment altogether for committing a far more serious offense.

Across much of Europe similar injustice prevailed until reformers spoke out.

One of the first to protest the existing conditions in Italy was the jurist and writer Cesare Bonesana Marchese di Beccaria. He was appalled by the deplorable conditions of the legal and judicial system in his country. All too often, he observed, those accused of crimes were denied due process of law or a fair trial. Officials frequently used torture to obtain confessions and then meted out cruel or excessive punishments. In Italy, for example, carrying a concealed weapon or illegally impersonating a priest were punishable by death.

Beccaria attacked these conditions in *An Essay on Crimes and Punishments,* published in 1764. He wrote that despite the many great accomplishments "of this enlightened age . . . the cruelty of punishments, and the irregularity of proceedings in criminal cases, so principal a part of the legislation, and so much neglected throughout Europe has hardly ever been called into question."[61]

Others across Europe joined Beccaria and demanded reform. They insisted that all legal code be based on reason, not the whims of kings, nobles, and priests, and applicable to everyone in society, commoners, merchants, priests, and nobles alike. Punishment for violating these laws, they said, should also be based on reason, not revenge. Penalties should be appropriate to the severity of the crime. Beccaria suggested that when considering the wide range of human misdeeds, lawmakers should use mathematical calculations to determine "a corresponding scale of punishments, descending from the greatest to the least."[62] He also wanted fair and open trials and the abolition of torture.

Beccaria's work was hugely influential and helped launch a widespread crusade that led to great improvement in the judicial systems of many European nations.

Humanitarianism

Concern for humanity, like that expressed by Beccaria, also convinced philosophes to attack the practice of slavery, which still existed in many European nations and their colonies around the world. In addition, they successfully fought to end the centuries-old practice of burning women suspected of being witches.

Humanitarianism also prompted many a public reconsideration of all women. Until the eighteenth century, European wo-

Cesare Bonesana Marchese di Beccaria criticized the legal and judicial systems of Italy. He advocated a system of laws based on reason, not the whims of nobility.

Beccaria Denounces Torture

An Essay on Crimes and Punishments, *written in 1764 by Italian economist and criminologist Cesare Bonesana Marchese di Beccaria, inspired the creation of humane penal codes across Europe. In this passage, taken from Lester G. Crocker's* The Age of Enlightenment, *Beccaria criticizes the use of torture to extract confessions.*

"The torture of a criminal, during the course of his trial, is a cruelty, consecrated by custom in most nations. It is used with an intent either to make him confess his crime, or explain some contradictions, into which he had been led during his examination; or to discover his accomplices; or . . . to discover other crimes, of which he is not accused, but of which he may be guilty.

No man can be judged a criminal until he be found guilty; nor can society take from him the public protection, until it has been proved that he has violated the conditions on which it was granted. What right, then, but that of power, can authorize the punishment of a citizen, so long as there remains any doubt of his guilt? The dilemma is frequent. Either he is guilty, or not guilty. If guilty, he should only suffer the punishment ordained by the laws, and torture becomes useless, as his confession is unnecessary. If he be not guilty, you torture the innocent; for, in the eye of the law, every man is innocent; whose crime has not been proved. Besides, it is confounding all relations, to expect that a man should be both the accuser and accused; and that pain should be the test of truth, as if truth resided in the muscles and fibres of a wretch in torture. By this method, the robust will escape, and the feeble be condemned. These are the inconveniences of this pretended test of truth, worthy only of a cannibal."

men, like their counterparts worldwide, had faced a multitude of indignities. In most European nations, they were confined to domestic duties, deprived of higher education, denied full employment opportunities, and accorded second-class citizen status.

Though the Enlightenment did not radically change these conditions, it did sow the seeds of slow change. Many essays demanding the emancipation of women appeared during the eighteenth century. In 1791 a woman French revolutionary, Olympe de Gouges, issued her own "Declaration of the Rights of Woman." In this document, she argues that women should have the same rights that men were then calling for:

A potential buyer examines slaves for sale. Enlightenment philosophes deplored the institution of slavery.

Woman is born free and lives equal to man in her rights. Social distinctions can be based only on the common utility. . . .

The law must be the expression of the general will; all female and male citizens must contribute either personally or through their representatives to its formation; it must be the same for all: male and female citizens, being equal in the eyes of the law, must be equally admitted to all honors, positions, and public employment according their capacity and without other distinctions besides those of their virtues and talents.[63]

But the Enlightenment also confused women. Reason suggested that all human beings had natural and equal rights, but by the end of the eighteenth century, the emphasis on sentiment produced an opposite effect. Women and men, insisted many proponents of sentiment, differed biologically and emotionally; therefore, they were different and should be treated accordingly.

Along with this reexamination of women came a change in attitudes toward marriage. Gradually, many Europeans came to accept the idea that women were partners in marriage, not the property of their husbands, as had been the traditional case in most nations.

Enlightened minds also focused on an even more vulnerable and overlooked group of human beings. Explains historian Peter Gay:

Children, too, and in the very century in which they were being exploited on farms and in factories, were discovered as human beings in their own rights. In the Middle Ages, through the sixteenth and seventeenth centuries, adults had treated children as toys, strange animals, or small grownups.[64]

Humanitarianism was also extended at long last to Europe's Jews, a despised religious and ethnic minority that had long been persecuted, unfairly taxed, and deprived of civil rights in most European countries. In 1720, John Toland, an English reformer, wrote an essay entitled *Reasons for Naturalising the Jews in Great Britain*

French revolutionary Olympe de Gouges rallied for women's rights. The Enlightenment's focus on human rights shed light on the legal inequality between men and women.

and Ireland. He argued that Jews ought to be granted the same rights as other British citizens. By the next century, Jews did receive these rights. Jews in the United States also received full equality. But when Joseph II of Austria tried to elevate the status of Jews in Prussia, the citizens of this German-speaking land resisted and prevented his decree from being successfully carried out.

Freedom of Thought

Philosophes believed the key to finding solutions to all the vexing problems of society rested within humanity itself. And the only way to arrive at these solutions was to allow freedom of expression without punishment, something most absolute monarchs and church officials opposed.

Having the liberty to express oneself, however, was considered a natural right by philosophes. They believed when citizens were able to comment openly and freely and reasonably on important issues a contest of ideas would occur. Out of these debates, philosophes hoped truth would prevail and enable society's leaders to make wiser decisions.

But philosophes also understood that for free speech to work well, citizens of a society must be tolerant of different views and beliefs. Voltaire summed up the thinking of many philosophes when he told a correspondent, "I detest what you write, but I would give my life to make it possible for you to continue to write."[65]

This concept was hard for many Europeans to accept, however. Some religious zealots, for instance, considered tolerance

Enlightenment Is Freedom

In Immanuel Kant's essay "What Is Enlightenment?" which appears in The Portable Enlightenment Reader, *edited by Isaac Kramnick, the famous German philosopher clarifies what he sees as the central goal of the Enlightenment.*

"Enlightenment is man's release from his . . . inability to make use of his understanding without direction from another. . . . Have courage to use your own reason! . . .

Laziness and cowardice are the reasons why so great a portion of mankind . . . remain . . . [under the direction of others] . . . and why it is so easy for others to set themselves up as their guardians. It is so easy not to . . . [think for yourself]. If I have a book which understands for me, a pastor who has a conscience for me, a physician who decides my diet, and so forth, I need not trouble myself. I need not think, if I can only pay—others will undertake the irksome work for me. . . .

For this enlightenment . . . nothing is required but freedom. . . . It is the freedom to make public use of one's reason at every point. But I hear on all sides, 'Do not argue!' The officer says: 'Do not argue but drill!' The tax collector: 'Do not argue but pay!' The cleric: 'Do not argue but believe!' Only one prince in the world says, 'Argue as much as you will, and about what you will, but obey!' Everywhere there is restriction of freedom. . . .

The public use of one's reason must always be free, and it alone can bring about enlightenment among men."

of different faiths to be a weakness. They believed God expected them to destroy or censor ideas that appeared to contradict the true faith.

Against such intolerance the philosophes made their stand. If nothing else, the Enlightenment became a battle to free the individual conscience from the powers of conformity, prejudice, and superstition.

Before its demise at the end of the eighteenth century, this long campaign for personal freedom, now based on reason and feeling, had spread farther than early philosophes had dreamed.

Chapter

6 The Rise and Fall of the Enlightenment

By the second half of the eighteenth century, the Enlightenment had traveled far beyond the borders of France. Talk of reason, progress, science, and freedom was heard from Scandinavia to Italy to North America, and even in relatively backward Russia.

Several forces propelled this expansion. A growing industrial revolution was now well under way across western Europe that spurred an intense curiosity about science, industry, inventions, and many other topics raised by the French encyclopedists. This rise in industry also created an expanding middle class whose annual income rivaled—and often surpassed—that of the aristocracy. To protect their economic gains, many in the middle class sought a greater role in government by supporting the economic and political reforms advocated by the philosophes.

Many of these new ideas appeared in learned journals published by numerous royal academies of science, medicine, literature, agriculture, art, and other fields that appeared in England, France, Sweden, Spain, Italy, Russia, and North America. These academies also encouraged essay contests, discussions, and debates on philosophical and academic topics.

Early book printers man the presses. The invention of the printing press led to the widespread publication of journals and books that advocated Enlightenment ideas.

Reading societies also played an important role in promoting the Enlightenment. For the most part, these groups had evolved from organizations set up during the seventeenth century to standardize the use of languages in Germany, Denmark, Sweden, and the Netherlands. By the eighteenth century they had a new mission—to promote the ideas of the Enlightenment through reading.

But the Enlightenment was not limited to readers of the educated upper classes. Europe's commoners were also keeping up with many of the new ideas thanks to a rise in literacy made possible by new circulating libraries and public schools that appeared in France, Germany, Britain, and elsewhere. As never before, new educational opportunities opened up to females, who made up Europe's majority and until now were often denied formal education past the elementary level.

The Enlightenment enjoyed a boost from an unlikely ally—the Protestant religious movement. An article of faith among Protestants was that all Christians had the right to read the Bible for themselves. This habit transferred readily to the reading of other literature.

Europe's growing literacy was further strengthened by a rising flood of new publications, ranging from the French *Encyclopedia* to pamphlets, brochures, periodicals, "moral weeklies," and books. Noted a German traveler in Paris:

> Everyone, especially the women, has a book in his pocket. Women, children, workmen, apprentices read in the shops. On Sundays the people who sit on their doorsteps read. Lackeys read behind coaches, coachmen up on their seats, soldiers at their quarters and *commissionnaires* at their posts.[66]

Along with Richard Steele, Joseph Addison (pictured) published the popular Spectator, *which featured articles and essays that advocated virtuous behavior and good manners.*

To make their ideas more appealing to general readers, many Enlightenment authors stopped using Latin, the language of scholars, and instead wrote in everyday, or vernacular, languages such as English, French, and German. By the end of the eighteenth century, the use of French was so widespread that it replaced Latin as Europe's international language.

The ability to read, however, did not assure that human minds became enlightened. Many of Europe's new readers, in fact, turned to cheap entertainments and pornographic literature rather than the more philosophical works of the Enlightenment. Undaunted, many philosophes believed they could raise the intellectual awareness of the common people through special periodicals that popularized weighty topics. The first of these appeared in Britain in the form of dailies and weeklies and then spread to the Continent. Though they varied in style, quality, and content, the periodicals generally took a lighthearted approach to matters of manners and morality. Many of them competed with printed sermons that were also for sale in the big cities.

The most popular periodical of all, and the one that set the standards for most of its competitors, was Joseph Addison's and Sir Richard Steele's *Spectator,* an English publication that first appeared in 1711. The *Spectator* featured articles and essays concerning the importance of philosophy, virtuous behavior, and good manners. Contributors to the publication often made these points by satirizing the bad manners and vulgarity of others. As historian John Gay observes:

Their very tone—their sweet reasonableness, their decent language, their gentle wit—was a rebuke to coarseness, an appeal . . . [to put aside party politics] . . . an invitation and a guide to gentlemanly conduct. . . . Their choice of expression . . . made them accessible to men and women with a modicum of learning.[67]

Addison Explains "The Aims of the Spectator."

In this passage from a March 12, 1711, essay in the Spectator, No. 10, *which appears in* The Norton Anthology of Literature, *Joseph Addison explains his goal to enlighten the readers of his periodical.*

"I . . . [calculate that I have 75,000 readers] . . . in London and Westminster, who I hope will take care to distinguish themselves from the thoughtless herd of their ignorant and unattentive . . . [fellow residents]. . . . I shall spare no pains to make their instruction agreeable, and their diversion useful. . . . I shall . . . [try to make moral issues interesting]. . . . And . . . I have resolved to refresh their memories from day to day, till I have recovered them out of that desperate state of vice and folly into which the age is fallen. The mind that lies fallow but a single day sprouts up in follies that are only to be killed by a constant and . . . [diligent] culture. . . . I shall be ambitious to have it said of me that I have brought philosophy out of closets and libraries, schools and colleges, to swell in clubs and assemblies, at tea tables and in coffeehouses."

The Power of Imitation

The Enlightenment's popularity among France's educated and privileged classes made it fashionable. In Paris, status-conscious noble ladies used the Enlightenment as a theme for gala social events. They frequently invited friends, acquaintances, travelers, and even philosophes themselves to their drawing rooms, or salons, to discuss literature, economics, politics, philosophy, and a host of other ideas.

At these extravagant affairs, guests were expected to exhibit not only cleverness, wit, and intelligence, but also graciousness, refinement, self-control, and polite manners. This emphasis on good manners became a major element of the Enlightenment and was copied by others across Europe. "Every man of any education would rather be called a rascal than accused of deficiency in the graces,"[68] observed eighteenth-century English author Samuel Johnson.

Since most Europeans lacked the social status to hope for an invitation to such

A literary circle in France discusses the latest philosophical ideas. Among France's educated class such gatherings, called salons, were formed to discuss ideas and to show off the guests' wit and intelligence.

a gathering, they did the next best thing by imitating the salons in their own social circles. Across Europe, and as far away as America, enthusiasts of the Enlightenment gathered in private homes, coffeehouses, courts, academies, and universities to emulate the salons of Paris.

The ideas of the Enlightenment filtered down to the working classes. Skilled craftsmen and household servants whose work put them in close contact with the upper classes were able to observe and copy the dress, language, and reading habits of their social betters.

Though some aristocrats and wealthy merchants resented being imitated, others encouraged the practice, especially those who honored the old European custom of noblesse oblige, or the obligation of the nobility to be generous and helpful to the less privileged.

Not all the proponents of the Enlightenment were so open in their actions. The new and often subversive material of the philosophes also held special appeal for those who practiced secrecy.

The Secret Advocates

One such secret organization was the Freemasons. Started in 1717, the Freemasons invoked the spirit of a much earlier brotherhood of bricklayers who built Europe's Christian cathedrals in the Middle Ages. They also used secret initiations, greetings, and symbols to create a bond of fellowship and friendship among a membership that included people of such diverse social backgrounds as Christians, Jews, workers, middle-class merchants, lesser nobles, and even clergymen.

According to their creed, "The Society of Freemasons has no aim other than to foster peace and harmony among men. Every civilized state should afford its members protection, if it is interested in its own welfare and happiness."[69] During the eighteenth century, Freemasons believed the key to such brotherhood lay in the ideals of the Enlightenment. At their numerous masonic lodge meetings across Europe, they urged their members to accept Deism, humanitarianism, science, reason, and other Enlightenment ideals.

Though their roots were ancient, the Freemasons also considered themselves important promoters of the Enlightenment. According to historian Ulrich Im Hof:

> The Freemasons were conscious of standing at a turning point where the middle ages . . . were giving way to the dawn of a new light. . . . The movement saw itself as rooted in very ancient Christian ideas; on the other hand, it stood for a modern, enlightened version of Christianity—or simply for a religion of Nature.[70]

In 1760 another secret society appeared in Bavaria, a region of southern Germany, that was even more determined than the Freemasons to promote the Enlightenment cause. Called the Illuminati, this mysterious fraternity intended to "see that light prevails." In addition, its members proclaimed, "We are warriors fighting against darkness, this is what we call the service of fire."[71]

To achieve their goals, the Illuminati was prepared to do more than discuss the Enlightenment. Its members, who included nobles, government officials, university professors, and clergymen, set out to gather as much information as possible about the workings of Germany's many local and

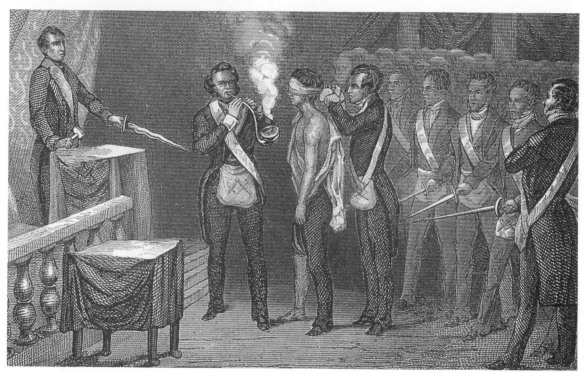

In a meeting of the Freemasons, an initiate is inducted in an elaborate ceremony. Freemasons prided themselves on advancing Enlightenment ideas.

regional governments and expose any practice they considered hopelessly encrusted with tradition and special privilege.

Enlightenment in Other Lands

Thus, a variety of factors spread the Enlightenment to parts of Europe and America. In each of these lands, it took on unique characteristics.

In Italy, for instance, the Enlightenment arrived thanks to a steady stream of visitors from England and France, along with the efforts of Italian Freemasons and the unstoppable appearance of the writings of the French philosophes. Although

the Catholic Church placed the works of Voltaire, Diderot, Rousseau, and others on its list of forbidden books, all were widely available anyway. For one thing, these authors could be read with special permission from church officials. Censors also had difficulty controlling what people read in Italy, a land of seaports and many travelers. Many of the forbidden works were easily imported from France. In some cases, the ideals of the Enlightenment appeared without much interference at all; Diderot's *Encyclopedia,* for example, was openly published in several Italian cities.

The Durants observe, "In a modest degree, in a form available for persons who read French, the Enlightenment reached Italy. But the Italians deliberately and for the most part contentedly refrained from philosophy."[72] Instead, they concentrated on music, art, and poetry to stimulate a vibrant intellectual life during the eighteenth century.

Though the Enlightenment was not robust in Italy, it did inspire many reforms. By the end of the eighteenth century, Italians saw many improvements in their daily lives. Thanks to Beccaria's influence, for instance, most Italian states reformed their legal codes by the end of the century. Other reforms, many initiated by Italy's powerful autocratic rulers, brought progress in tax equality, a reduction in the power and wealth of the church, and the abolition of many special privileges enjoyed by the nobility.

In 1783, Pietro Tambirini, an Italian Catholic priest, published "On Ecclesiastical and Civil Toleration," an essay denouncing the Inquisition, the Catholic Church's centuries-old official tribunal that persecuted freethinkers. Other critics also spoke out and by the end of the eighteenth century, the Inquisition was disappearing. By 1809 it was officially abolished everywhere in Italy.

Censorship and persecution also made it hard for the Enlightenment to take root in Catholic Spain. Nonetheless, many men and women across the country secretly read works of the philosophes that were smuggled into the country. Here and there, many Spaniards formed organizations called

On Thinking Clearly

In his book Philosophical Dictionary, *published in 1764, Voltaire recommends "rules for the direction of the mind." This sampling of his idea appears in* Voltaire *by Peyton E. Richter and Ilona Ricardo.*

"1. We must repeat what Locke has so strongly urged—*Define your terms.* . . . The abuse of words is an inexhaustible subject. In history, in morality, in jurisprudence, in medicine, but especially in theology, beware of . . . [lack of clarity].

2. We ought often to be very uncertain of what we are certain of; and we may fail in good sense when deciding according to what is called *common* sense.

3. There are two ways of being deceived; by false judgment and self-blindness—that of erring like a man of genius, and that of deciding like a fool. . . .

4. Disgust with our own existence, weariness of ourselves, is a malady which is likewise a cause of suicide. The remedy is a little exercise, music, hunting, the play, or an agreeable woman. The man who, in a fit of melancholy, kills himself today, would have wished to live had he waited a week."

Sociedades Económicas de los Amigos del País (Economic Societies of the Friends of the Country) that encouraged open discussion of the ideas of the Enlightenment. They also set up schools and libraries to promote education and literacy. By 1759, Spain even had its own enlightened despot, Charles III, who managed to weaken church control of both the courts and education, set up land reforms that enabled many poor people to own property, and create a network of new roads and canals.

Russia's monarch, Catherine the Great, also fancied herself an enlightened ruler. An admirer and correspondent of several philosophes, she set out to improve Russian society. Inspired by Beccaria's essay on legal reform, she abolished torture and established religious toleration in her empire. At her insistence, the Russian government set up new elementary and high schools for her subjects, as well as a teachers' college, the first ever for women. She also forced the powerful Russian Orthodox Church to recognize that it was subservient to the government.

Shocked by the poor quality of health of the people in her empire, Catherine opened new hospitals and asylums, imported foreign doctors, founded a medical college, and introduced inoculations for smallpox into Russia. She also advocated the Enlightenment ideas of liberty and equality, though in her view equality merely meant that all citizens had to obey the same laws, and liberty gave them only the right to do what the laws permitted.

Another enlightened despot was Joseph II, whose empire included Austria, Hungary, the southern Netherlands, and Bohemia, a region of Czechoslovakia. Joseph believed a modern empire required a government run by educated professionals that worked with the efficiency and precision of Newton's universe. A careful student of his people's problems, Joseph implemented several reforms. He abolished serfdom, created a fairer tax system, made improvements in the educational system, established the principle of equality before the law, and set up a national court system. Capital punishment was abolished. So too were church-run courts. No longer did the government punish those who practiced magic or witchcraft. Joseph closed some monasteries and convents because he believed they were not contributing to society; he also required bishops to take an oath of loyalty to the government.

In 1781 he decreed that his government stood for religious tolerance. Joseph

Inspired by the Enlightenment, Catherine the Great of Russia reformed many of her country's institutions, including opening new hospitals, abolishing torture, and establishing religious tolerance.

later explained his actions to a nobleman: "Intolerance is banished from my Empire. . . . Toleration is the effect of the propagation of the enlightenment which has now spread through all Europe. It is based on philosophy, and on the great men who have established it. . . . It is philosophy that governments must follow."[73]

The Aufklärung: Germany's Enlightenment

Conditions in Germany during the eighteenth century were less hospitable to the arrival of the Enlightenment than elsewhere. Unlike England and France, Germany was not a unified nation. Instead, it was a fragmented realm of over three hundred separate states. It did not yet have a strong middle class trying to wrest power from kings and nobles. Industrialization was also far less advanced in Germany than in England and France. Finally, Germans were not as dissatisfied with organized religion as the French were. Nor were they as impressed with the ideas of using reason and the scientific method to analyze social problems as were their counterparts in England.

Nonetheless, the spirit of Enlightenment did come to Germany. In Prussia, a region of northern Germany, many reforms were enacted by another enlightened despot, Frederick II, also known as Frederick the Great. A witty, intelligent, serious student of the Enlightenment, he spent years studying the problems of his nation and hearing complaints from his subjects. In response, he reduced the use of torture, allowed freedom of the press, combined all Prussian laws into one code,

Frederick the Great reduced the use of torture, reformed Prussia's law codes, and allowed a free press.

and reformed his government's civil service by trying to make it more efficient. He also granted Catholics equal status with Protestants, though Poles and Jews still faced discrimination.

Elsewhere in Germany, many intellectuals fell under the spell of several of France's philosophes. Some scholars were so captivated, in fact, that in addition to Latin, they expressed their ideas in French rather than their native German in both books and lectures.

The French influence eventually faded, however. As skepticism and the spirit of inquiry grew in Germany, thinkers and writers questioned their country's reliance on foreign cultural influences. Increasingly, Germany's intellectuals demanded that the Aufklärung, as the Enlightenment was called in Germany, reflect their own culture.

A leading proponent of this idea was Gottfried Wilhelm Leibniz, a multitalented writer who, along with other German intellectuals, urged German-speaking peoples to take pride in their own culture. Another reformer, scholar, and professor, Christian Thomasius, caused a stir simply by lecturing to his classes in German rather than Latin.

Many young German writers took up the banner of German pride. By the 1750s they were producing poems, plays, and other writings with an overt emphasis on German culture. Thanks to these voices and others, the Aufklärung developed a strong sense of national pride, a characteristic much less detectable in France.

But this nationalistic trend did not satisfy a group of young German intellectuals who belonged to a submovement within the Aufklärung called Sturm und Drang (Storm and Stress). These rebels complained that the Enlightenment was too optimistic. Instead, they preferred to dwell on the so-called dark side of the German soul, a melancholy spirit that has appeared in German literature for centuries. Advocates of Sturm und Drang also celebrated personal strength and power in their writings. Freedom from all restraints in society, not the reason and order of the French philosophes, was their goal.

As Germany's Aufklärung evolved into something quite different from what many philosophes had envisioned, the Enlightenment's original thrust was very much alive elsewhere—in far-off America.

Gottfried Leibniz advocated that Germans stop taking on Enlightenment ideas from foreign nations and begin to form their own ideas based on reason.

The Enlightenment in America

Despite their considerable distance from Europe, many Americans were charmed by the ideas of the philosophes. Though they had no royal courts and no salons to promote the Enlightenment, Americans did have bustling towns and cities that welcomed and nurtured new ideas. Philadelphia, a young cosmopolitan city that boasted a university, a medical center, and many scientific and philosophical clubs, became the center of the American Enlightenment.

Here too was the home of America's greatest Enlightenment figure, Benjamin Franklin. "Printer, journalist, scientist, politician, diplomat, educator, statesman, author . . . he was, or seemed, the complete philosophe, American style, as representative of his nation as Voltaire was of France, or Goethe of Germany,"[74] writes historian Henry Steele Commager.

The revolutionary spirit that eventually caused Americans to break from British rule was also greatly inspired by the Enlightenment. According to Peter Gay, "[The early revolutionaries] sprinkled their inflammatory writings with ideas, arguments, and phrases, borrowed from writers of the Enlightenment."[75]

Many Americans in fact saw nothing wrong with their rebellion against the Brit-

Benjamin Franklin was one of many American revolutionaries who were Deists. Remnants of Deist ideas can be found in the U.S. Constitution.

ish king. In their view, they were wisely following the ideas of Locke and Rousseau, whose influence is evident in the nation's Declaration of Independence:

> We hold these truths to be self-evident, that all men are created equal, that they are endowed by the Creator with certain unalienable rights, that among these are Life, Liberty and the pursuit of Happiness. That to secure these rights, Governments are instituted among Men, deriving their just Powers from the consent of the governed. That whenever any Form of Government become destructive of these ends, it is the Right of the People to alter or to abolish it, and to institute new Government.[76]

Enlightenment principles were also enshrined in the U.S. Constitution. This document reveals that Americans shared Britain's preference for divided power; it establishes a government with executive, legislative, and judicial branches. The Constitution also provides a system of checks and balances to keep any one branch from becoming too powerful.

Deism also found a home in America. Thomas Jefferson, Benjamin Franklin, James Madison, Thomas Paine, and many others of the nation's founding fathers believed in some type of natural religion. Traces of Deist thought appear in several of the nation's cherished documents. The Declaration of Independence, for example, contains a reference to the "God of Nature," not a biblical one. The Articles of Confederation, which specified the nation's form of government before the adoption of the Constitution, calls God the "Great Governor of the World." The Constitution does not mention God at all.

The United States, in fact, may have been the Enlightenment's greatest achievement. "The Old World imagined, invented and formulated the Enlightenment, the New World . . . realized it and fulfilled it,"[77] notes Henry Steele Commager.

Most likely this outcome was possible because America's unique situation made it highly receptive to the ideas of the philosophes. Unlike Europeans, Americans did not experience periods of bloody religious persecution. Nor were they hostile to organized religion. In America religion was largely a private, not public, matter. Americans had no state religion, as in England. The idea of separation of church and state had widespread support in the New World.

At first only aristocrats and highly educated Americans were attracted to the Enlightenment. Eventually, though, the nation's common people also embraced many of the ideas. America's working classes, after all, were more apt than their European counterparts to use reason in their daily lives. They had a wilderness to tame. This meant they were constantly setting up new dwellings, farms, communities, churches, transportation systems, and businesses. All these efforts required a multitude of problem-solving strategies based on reason and practicality. Government leaders in the New World especially welcomed any new insights on social and economic matters that could assist them in creating a new society.

At the same time, American manufacturers came to appreciate new ideas in science and technology. Many, for example, were keenly interested in new machinery that would enable them to harness America's abundant water power for industrial purposes. They also wanted to study the modern factory system, which with its new machinery and efficient division of labor seemed to many observers a proud example of the Enlightenment at its best.

Another factor that helped open American minds to the Enlightenment was its social structure. During the eighteenth century, European society was rigidly fixed in a way that constantly favored the nobility and clergy and left little room for anyone else at the top. To a much greater degree, America rewarded its high achievers blessed with talent and merit—that is, as long as they were white males.

Many Enlightenment ideas found their expression in the U.S. Declaration of Independence, including the idea that the government must serve the people.

Two Enlightened Worlds

The influence of the Enlightenment on both sides of the Atlantic Ocean is evident in both the Virginia Bill of Rights of 1776 and the French Constitution of 1791. This comparison originally appears in Democracy in Germany: History and Perspectives, *published by the Federal Republic of Germany.*

The Virginia Bill of Rights of 1776

All men are by nature equally free and independent.

All power is vested in the people and consequently is derived from them. Officials are their trustees and servants and are at all times responsible to them.

The Legislative and Executive powers of the State should be separate and distinct from the Judiciative.

Freedom of the Press is one of the greatest bulwarks of liberty and can never be restrained but by despotic governments.

The French Constitution of 1791

Men are born and remain free and equal in rights.

The principle of all sovereignty resides essentially in the nation. No body nor individual may exercise authority which does not proceed directly from the nation.

A society in which the . . . separation of powers is not defined, has no constitution at all.

The free communication of ideas and opinions is one of the most precious rights of man. Every citizen may accordingly speak, write and print with freedom but shall be responsible for such abuses of this freedom defined by law.

Europeans noticed these developments in the New World and were generally pleased. Many looked on America as the Enlightenment's best hope of success. The French philosophe marquis de Condorcet called it "the most enlightened, the freest, and the least burdened by prejudices"[78] of all other nations.

And as Americans fashioned their new nation on the principles of the Enlighten-

ment, they were themselves fashioned into promoters of their own brand of Enlightenment. As historian Peter Gay notes, "The American Revolution converted America from an importer of ideas into an exporter. What it exported was, of course, . . . the program of enlightenment in practice."[79]

Among those who imported this American program were French radicals who decided that at last the time had come to wipe out the ancien régime forever.

The Enlightenment's Twilight Years

By the 1780s the French national government was on the verge of bankruptcy. Nobles and church officials clung to their special privileges and the monarchy failed to realize the seriousness of public discontent. Much of this dissatisfaction had been whipped up by the philosophes' criticism of France's social ills. In addition, France now suffered acute food shortages, high prices, and mass unemployment. Frustrated by the lack of progress in addressing their nation's vexing problems, the French people finally turned to radical means; in 1789 they rose up in revolt.

Most of the philosophes, including Voltaire and Rousseau, were now dead. Nonetheless, the power of their ideas lived on. Though the Enlightenment cannot be called the direct cause of the French Revolution, it did contribute to the intellectual climate and the type of leaders who emerged to lead the Revolution. "If the first phase of the Revolution, from 1789 to 1791, was not directly caused by the Enlightenment, it nevertheless transferred political power in France to the men who had been most influenced by the Enlightenment,"[80] writes historian Norman Hampson.

During this first phase of the Revolution, the ancien régime came to an end. A new government, the National Assembly, convened and passed many new laws that appeared to have flowed from the pens of the philosophes themselves. All special church privileges were abolished. Payments of tithes and other fees to the Catholic Church were stopped. All traces of feudalism were abolished. Titles and class distinctions were outlawed. All citizens were declared equal before the law and were eligible to run for public office. The National Assembly also lifted guild restrictions on manufacturing and trade.

In addition, the new lawmakers crafted a document that spelled out guidelines for a new French society. The Declaration of the Rights of Man and the Citizen, influenced by the writings of the philosophes, the English Bill of Rights, and the U.S. Constitution, proclaimed that the French people were free and entitled to equal rights, including the right to exercise freedom of speech and the press, own property, make laws, and hold opinions and religious beliefs immune from persecution.

In 1791 the National Assembly also set up plans for a constitutional monarchy and adopted a new constitution that teemed with principles of the Enlightenment. During July of this same year, government leaders ordered that Voltaire's body be exhumed from Champagne and brought to Paris and buried at a national cemetery for French heroes. His remains, along with portraits of both Voltaire and Rousseau, were paraded through the streets of Paris lined with crowds of people wanting to pay their respects to the "fathers of the Revolution." On Voltaire's sarcophagus were inscribed the words, "Poet, philosopher, historian, he caused the human spirit to take a great leap forward, he prepared us to be free."[81]

Three years later Rousseau's remains were transferred from the Isle of Poplars in France and laid to rest not far from Voltaire's.

Though many French people believed the Revolution was now over, this was not to be the case. Fierce opposition to the new revolutionary government mounted and forged a new round of political crises. In 1793 the Revolution entered a new and bloodier phase when an extremely radical faction took control of the movement and imposed a murderous regime known as the Reign of Terror.

Fanatics were now in charge. Under their orders, thousands were beheaded by a new killing machine called the guillotine. Many nobles were executed. So too was anyone who disagreed in any way with the new government. Even those who objected to the executions were likewise destroyed. As author T. Z. Lavine explains:

Rather than the truths of reason, the voice of the people became the sole source of truth. The enemy to be destroyed was not false beliefs, but any individual persons or political groups who seemed to oppose the will of the people. This was the Reign of Terror, in which the Revolution devoured its own leaders, one of the bloodiest scenes of horror and violence in European history.[82]

Revolutionaries also carried out a fierce anti-Christian campaign that reduced church officials to humiliated servants of the new government. France's zealous leaders eradicated the Christian calendar and adopted a new one. The Year One marked the Revolution's start. Some

The French peasantry take up arms against the nobility. Although based on Enlightenment ideas, the French Revolution descended into mindless violence.

radicals converted Paris's famed cathedral, Notre Dame, into one of the nation's new Temples of Reason where French citizens were encouraged to mock religion and celebrate the Feast of Reason.

The Revolution traumatized France and most of the rest of Europe. A government led by power-hungry extremists who terrorized and executed their fellow citizens in the name of reason and progress was never the intent of the Enlightenment. Philosophes had always opposed war and mass murder. They favored reform through government and law, not the barrel of a gun. Their dream was a society based on reason; what the Revolution produced instead was irrationality. They wanted enlightened government; instead they received murderous mob rule. Worse yet, the Revolution paved the way for the rise of a military dictator—

An opponent of the Reign of Terror is led to the guillotine. The excesses of the French Revolution terrified people throughout the world.

Napoléon Bonaparte—whose rule was as tyrannical as that of France's kings.

The French Revolution terrified Europeans everywhere who believed upheaval and anarchy would spread to their own nations. By now many considered the Enlightenment as a big mistake and blamed it for the downfall of tradition, law, and order. In their eyes, the philosophes had set in motion a cold, soulless, atheistic force that threatened to destroy stability and authority everywhere. In fact, after Napoléon took power in 1799 and later invaded his European neighbors he was resisted by opponents who saw themselves fighting "against the Enlightenment which they had come to identify with the Revolution and the upstart Emperor,"[83] writes Norman Hampson.

Many French leaders also voiced hatred of all traces of the Enlightenment. The comte de Montlosier, a supporter of monarchy, said it was necessary to march "well armed, and if possible with heavy artillery, against anything which nowadays calls itself spread of enlightenment, progress of civilization, spirit of the age."[84] Some critics so distrusted the Enlightenment that they publicly railed against what they saw as an excess of books and schools in France.

Having reached its zenith in the late eighteenth century, the Enlightenment soon became overshadowed by new movements such as Romanticism, which emphasized tradition, instinct, emotion, and intuition and expressed distrust of reason. And by the early nineteenth century, the Enlightenment had clearly faded as Europe's most powerful source of intellectual stimulation.

But the legacy of the Enlightenment did not stop. It lingered on steadily for more than two centuries.

7 The Legacy of the Enlightenment

The ideas enshrined by the Enlightenment were so powerful and durable that not even the calamity of the French Revolution could permanently silence them. Their legacy remains today a big part of modern life.

Freedom, democracy, tolerance, humanitarianism, human rights, and a belief that the acquisition of knowledge, science, and technology lead to progress of the human condition are all the hallmarks of Western European and North American culture. All these notions grew out of the Enlightenment.

Reason and sentimentalism created a spirit of compassion in the eighteenth century that brought an end to the era of burning witches and torturing prisoners. Slavery began its slow demise in the wake of the Enlightenment. Foundling homes for abandoned children were opened. New hospitals were set up for the mentally ill, who were treated there as patients rather than demon possessed. Jails improved and trials became fairer. But there was also another lasting change in the legal system. As historian Isaac Kramnick puts it, because of the Enlightenment, "Public law no longer enforced God's higher truths nor any ideal of the moral life; it merely kept order."[85]

The illumination of the Enlightenment permanently altered how Europeans and North Americans viewed their relationships with their fellow citizens. No longer did they accept the ancient idea of the "great chain of being." The Enlightenment destroyed the old notion that a European's main purpose in life was to serve as obedient subject to an absolute monarch or a dogmatic church. Instead, a new concept prevailed that each man, woman, and child was a unique being, entitled to inalienable rights that no one had the right to violate.

Other legacies of the Enlightenment are evident in modern schools and universities. Today's social sciences—sociology, psychology, political science, economics, anthropology, and comparative religions—all trace their origins to the early attempts of the philosophes to employ reason and empiricism to explain the workings of the human mind and the institutions of society.

The Impact of the Enlightenment on the Arts

The Enlightenment even touched the arts. Many artists, designers, musicians, and writers of the eighteenth century admired both the form and grace of ancient Rome and the Enlightenment's emphasis on rules, convention, and mathematical precision.

An English scientist performs an electrical experiment for members of the Royal Society. The Enlightenment inspired such scientific societies.

But the tradition-breaking spirit of the Enlightenment also inspired many composers and musicians to seek new forms of expression. Earlier in the seventeenth century, most musical compositions were religious in nature and performed in cathedrals and churches. But during the Enlightenment, increasingly secular musical compositions were being enjoyed in theaters and other nonreligious settings. True to the spirit of the Enlightenment, Austrian composer Franz Joseph Haydn infused a passion for nature into his sonatas, quartets, and other musical compositions.

Another great enthusiast of the Enlightenment was German composer Wolfgang Amadeus Mozart. Observes historian Isaac Kramnick:

> Few have captured the spirit of the Enlightenment, its intellectual and social agenda, as has Mozart in his opera, *The*

Magic Flute, with its secular priests presiding over Temples of Wisdom, Reason, and Nature, is a series of variations on the triumph of light over darkness, of sun over moon, of day over night, of reason, tolerance, and love over passion, hate, and revenge.[86]

Literature

Fiction writers also wove Enlightenment themes into their works. In Great Britain, many authors followed the example of Rousseau and explored not only sentiment but also the psychology of men and women in their books. Laurence Sterne's novel *Tristram Shandy,* published in 1760, introduced a literary technique that explored the thinking process of the characters.

Many writers also turned away from the traditional methods of storytelling that focused primarily on the exploits of ancient warriors and kings. Instead, they portrayed common, realistic everyday characters who became involved in a variety of experiences. In his 1749 novel *Tom Jones,* English author Henry Fielding presents a full canvas of characters in British society, not merely the high and mighty. Such literary traditions are vigorous today.

The Writing of History

The Enlightenment also transformed the way history was written. Previously, much of what passed for history was pure speculation and opinion. Historians of the Middle Ages often reported various historical

Musicians, too, were inspired by the Enlightenment, including composer Wolfgang Amadeus Mozart.

On the Mathematical Principles of Music

Jean-Philippe Rameau's infatuation with the guiding influence of reason (in the form of mathematics) on musical composition is apparent in this excerpt from an essay that appears in The Enlightenment: The Culture of the Eighteenth Century, *edited by Isidor Schneider.*

"Music is a science which ought to have certain rules. These rules should be derived from a self-evident principle which cannot become known to us without the help of mathematics. I must concede that despite all the experience I acquired in music through its practice over a considerable period of time, it was only with the help of mathematics that I was able to unravel my ideas, that light replaced an obscurity I had previously not recognized as such. . . . The true sense of these rules . . . developed with so much clarity and precision in my mind that I could not avoid concluding that it would be most desirable to have the musical knowledge of this century's composers equal their capacity to create beauty."

events as divinely inspired. They also tended to eulogize or flatter powerful authority figures such as kings, queens, and popes rather than portray them as human beings with both strengths and weaknesses.

But under the spell of the Enlightenment, a new generation of historians looked more deeply into the causes of great human events. Voltaire and other writers attempted to explain these occurrences as the consequences of human motives and powerful social, economic, and political forces.

In his masterpiece, *The Decline and Fall of the Roman Empire,* which appeared in 1776, English historian Edward Gibbon argued that Christianity and invading barbarians—and not God's wrath, as many had claimed—caused the fall of the great Roman Empire.

The new breed of Enlightenment historians was not always objective, however. Swayed by the Enlightenment, many tried to use historical events to prove that humanity was steadily making progress through the ages, a controversial yet very popular idea in the eighteenth century.

Critics of the Enlightenment

Despite its many achievements, the Enlightenment has evoked criticism through the ensuing two centuries. Many commentators have accused the philosophes of having set into motion an anarchic force that damaged humanity's traditional sources of authority, stability, and order. "Being segregated from the common man, they failed to realize that their doctrines, if pushed to logical conclusions, would create among the masses bewilderment and ever worse,"[87] observes Harold Nicolson.

Some critics also claim that the Enlightenment contributed to a feeling of despair, lack of meaning, and loneliness that typifies the modern age. They argue that the Enlightenment placed too much emphasis on individual rights rather than on personal responsibilities and community involvement. Furthermore, the philosophes stand accused of eroding the authority of religion and a belief in God, but offering nothing as a replacement to meet most people's spiritual needs.

The legacy of the Enlightenment even displeases some environmentalists who say that its stress on progress and reason has contributed to a contemporary materialistic approach to dealing with the natural world that has resulted in wholesale environmental destruction.

An unsigned essay in the *Economist* sums up the main arguments of those in the anti-Enlightenment camp:

> By rejecting all authority but reason, the Enlightenment left wickedness unchecked. By seeking to justify morality exclusively in terms of reason, man . . . [separated] ethics from knowledge. . . . He once sought to be wise, now he sought only to know. He worshipped not God but technology, and sacrificed his fellow man to it. Industrial dehumanization, concentration camps, atomic bombs: these were the fruits of knowledge without morals.[88]

The Enlightenment's Defenders Respond

Defenders of the Enlightenment think such attacks are harsh and largely undeserved. They make the point that philo-

How History Repeats Itself

In his book Enquiry Concerning Human Understanding, *published in 1748, British historian and philosopher David Hume expresses his belief that history provides a guide to understanding the present, in the same way that observations of the natural world reveal the laws of nature. This passage is quoted in* The Portable Enlightenment Reader.

"It is . . . [widely believed] that there is a great [sameness] . . . among the actions of men, in all nations and ages, and that human nature remains still the same . . . [in how it behaves]. The same motives always produce the same actions: The same events follow from the same causes. Ambition, avarice, self-love, vanity, friendship, generosity, public spirit: these passions . . . [in varying degrees] . . . have been, from the beginning of the world, and still are, the source of all the actions and enterprises which have ever been observed . . . [in human beings]. . . .

Mankind are so much the same, in all times and places that history informs us of nothing new or strange in this particular. Its chief use is only to discover the constant and universal principles of human nature, by showing men in all varieties of circumstances and situations, and furnishing us with materials from which we may form our observations and become acquainted with the regular springs of human actions and behavior. These records or wars, intrigues, factions, and revolutions, are so many collections of experiments, by which the politician or moral philosopher . . . [sets up] . . . the principles of his . . . [field of study] in the same manner as . . . [those who scientifically study the natural world]."

sophes certainly had their faults, but that in the long run their legacy has generated more good than bad for humanity.

Though reason and the scientific method did not erase all social ills of the eighteenth century, they did provide an effective way of studying social, economic, and political problems that is still used in the modern world.

Advocates of the Enlightenment tend to discount the French Revolution as a symbol of its shortcomings. In an essay titled "On the Influence of Enlightenment on Revolutions," writer and editor Johann Heinrich Tieftrunk made the following argument in 1794:

The history of every age gives us examples of revolution which were made possible only by the lack of enlightenment. France itself—had it been truly enlightened—would have either never

An early scientist experiments with plants in a laboratory at his home. The ideas of the Enlightenment forever changed Western culture.

have begun its revolution or else certainly have carried it out better.[89]

Many modern writers agree with this assessment. They point out that the Enlightenment must be considered in context. What the philosophes were reacting against were the enormous social, political, and economic ills of their own era. Their hope for the future was for a better world, one based on reason, sentiment, and respect for the individual.

Harvard professor Edward O. Wilson sums up their contribution:

The Enlightenment . . . brought the Western mind to the threshold of a new freedom. It waved aside everything, every form of religious and civil authority, every imaginable fear, to give precedence to the ethic of free inquiry. It pictured a universe in which humanity plays the role of perpetual adventurer. For two centuries God seemed to speak in a new voice to humankind.[90]

For better and for worse, that voice still speaks.

Notes

Introduction: Casting Light upon Darkness

1. Quoted in Norman Hampson, *The Enlightenment*. Baltimore: Penguin Books, 1968, p. 158.

2. William H. McNeil, *The Rise of the West*. Chicago: University of Chicago Press, 1963, p. 684.

3. Louis I. Bredvold, *The Brave New World of the Enlightenment*. Ann Arbor: University of Michigan Press, 1961, p. 1.

Chapter 1: The Roots of the Enlightenment

4. Quoted in Isaac Kramnick, ed., *The Portable Enlightenment Reader*. New York: Penguin Books, 1995, p. 5.

5. Isaiah Berlin, *The Age of Enlightenment: The 18th Century Philosophers*. New York: New American Library, 1956, p. 14.

6. Quoted in Ulrich Im Hof, *The Enlightenment*, trans. William E. Yuill. Oxford: Blackwell, 1994, p. 4.

7. Quoted in T. Z. Lavine, *From Socrates to Sartre: The Philosophic Quest*. New York: Bantam, 1984, p. 137.

8. Quoted in Will and Ariel Durant, *The Age of Louis XIV*, vol. VIII of *The Story of Civilization*. New York: Simon and Schuster, 1963, p. 581.

9. Quoted in George Seldes, ed., *The Great Thoughts*. New York: Ballantine, 1985, p. 104.

10. Quoted in Will and Ariel Durant, *The Age of Voltaire*, vol. IX of *The Story of Civilization*. New York: Simon and Schuster, 1965, p. 143.

11. Quoted in Christopher Hibber, ed., *Twilight of Princes*. New York: Newsweek Books, 1974, p. 63.

Chapter 2: The Rise of the French Philosophes

12. Quoted in Lester G. Crocker, ed., *The Age of Enlightenment*. New York: Walker, 1969, p. 2.

13. Quoted in Kramnick, *The Portable Enlightenment Reader*, p. 1.

14. Quoted in Durant, *The Age of Louis XIV*, p. 605.

15. Quoted in Durant, *The Age of Louis XIV*, p. 608.

16. Durant, *The Age of Louis XIV*, p. 613.

17. Quoted in Durant, *The Age of Louis XIV*, p. 609.

18. Quoted in Durant, *The Age of Louis XIV*, p. 610.

19. Quoted in Harold Nicolson, *The Age of Reason: The Eighteenth Century*. Garden City, NY: Doubleday, 1960, p. 42.

20. Quoted in Nicolson, *The Age of Reason*, p. 42.

21. Durant, *The Age of Louis XIV*, p. 613.

22. Nicolson, *The Age of Reason*, p. 89.

23. Quoted in Seldes, *The Great Thoughts*, p. 434.

24. Quoted in Peyton E. Richter and Ilona Ricardo, *Voltaire*. Boston: Twayne, 1980, p. 40.

25. Quoted in Seldes, *The Great Thoughts*, p. 434.

26. Quoted in Isidor Schneider, ed., *The Enlightenment: The Culture of the Eighteenth Century*. New York: George Braziller, 1965, p. 50.

27. Crocker, ed., *The Age of Enlightenment*, p. 2.

Chapter 3: The Attack on Christianity

28. Quoted in Peter Gay, *The Enlightenment: An Interpretation, vol. 2, The Science of Freedom*. New York: Knopf, 1969, p. 16.

29. Frank E. Manuel, ed., *The Enlightenment*. Englewood Cliffs, NJ: Prentice-Hall, 1965, p. 9.

30. Bredvold, *The Brave New World of the Enlightenment*, p. 137.

31. Quoted in M. H. Abrams, ed., *The Norton Anthology of English Literature,* vol. 1. New York: W. W. Norton, 1968, p. 1,726.

32. Quoted in Seldes, *The Great Thoughts,* p. 207.

33. Quoted in Durant, *The Age of Voltaire,* p. 609.

34. Quoted in Lavine, *From Socrates to Sartre,* p. 189.

35. Quoted in Seldes, *The Great Thoughts,* p. 15.

36. Quoted in Richter and Ricardo, *Voltaire,* p. 106.

37. Quoted in Hampson, *The Enlightenment,* p. 94.

38. Quoted in Crocker, *The Age of Enlightenment,* p. 162.

39. Quoted in Durant, *The Age of Voltaire,* p. 757.

Chapter 4: Revolt Against Reason

40. Quoted in Hampson, *The Enlightenment,* p. 193.

41. Quoted in Hampson, *The Enlightenment,* p. 195.

42. Quoted in Will and Ariel Durant, *Rousseau and Revolution,* vol. X of *The Story of Civilization.* New York: Simon and Schuster, 1967, p. 22.

43. Quoted in Nicolson, *The Age of Reason,* p. 417.

44. Jean-Jacques Rousseau, *The Social Contract.* Danbury, CT: Classics Appreciation Society, a Division of Grolier, 1957, p. 343.

45. Rousseau, *The Social Contract,* p. 352.

46. Rousseau, *The Social Contract,* p. 352.

47. Rousseau, *The Social Contract,* p. 354.

48. Quoted in Seldes, *The Great Thoughts,* p. 356.

49. Arthur J. May, *A History of Civilization: The Story of Our Heritage,* vol. 2, *The Mid–Seventeenth Century to Modern Times.* New York: Charles Scribner's Sons, 1964, p. 180.

50. Peter Gay and the Editors of Time-Life Books, *Age of Enlightenment,* New York: Time-Life, 1966, p. 77.

51. Quoted in Hampson, *The Enlightenment,* p. 119.

52. Bredvold, *The Brave New World of the Enlightenment,* p. 65.

53. Quoted in Nicolson, *The Age of Reason,* p. 381.

54. Quoted in Lavine, *From Socrates to Sartre,* p. 197.

Chapter 5: The Campaign to Reform Society

55. Quoted in Seldes, *The Great Thoughts,* p. 341.

56. Quoted in Seldes, *The Great Thoughts,* p. 108.

57. Quoted in Manuel, *The Enlightenment,* p. 117.

58. Quoted in Durant, *Rousseau and Revolution,* p. 143.

59. Quoted in Manuel, *The Enlightenment,* p. 106.

60. Quoted in Durant, *Rousseau and Revolution,* p. 76.

61. Quoted in Manuel, *The Enlightenment,* p. 140.

62. Quoted in Manuel, *The Enlightenment,* p. 142.

63. Quoted in Steven L. Jantzen, Larry S. Krieger, and Kenneth Neill, *World History: Perspectives on the Past.* Lexington, MA: D. C. Heath, 1992, p. 488.

64. Quoted in Gay, *The Enlightenment,* pp. 34–35.

65. Quoted in Seldes, *The Great Thoughts,* p. 434.

Chapter 6: The Rise and Fall of the Enlightenment

66. Quoted in Hampson, *The Enlightenment,* p. 138.

67. Gay, *The Enlightenment,* p. 53.

68. Quoted in Gay, *The Enlightenment,* p. 42.

69. Quoted in Im Hof, *The Enlightenment,* p. 141.

70. Im Hof, *The Enlightenment,* p. 141.

71. Quoted in Im Hof, *The Enlightenment,* p. 258.

72. Durant, *Rousseau and Revolution,* p. 220.

73. Quoted in Durant, *Rousseau and Revolution,* p. 357.

74. Henry Steele Commager, *The Empire of Reason: How Europe Imagined and America Realized the Enlightenment.* Garden City, NY: Anchor Press/Doubleday, 1977, p. 19.

75. Gay, *The Enlightenment,* p. 558.

76. Quoted in John M. Blum et al., *The National Experience: A History of the United States,* 6th ed. San Diego: Harcourt Brace Jovanovich, 1985, p. 922.

77. Commager, *The Empire of Reason,* p. xi.

78. Quoted in Kramnick, *The Portable Enlightenment Reader,* p. xviii.

79. Gay, *The Enlightenment,* p. 558.

80. Hampson, *The Enlightenment,* p. 256.

81. Quoted in Richter and Ricardo, *Voltaire,* p. 44.

82. Lavine, *From Socrates to Sartre,* p. 190.

83. Hampson, *The Enlightenment,* p. 263.

84. Quoted in Hampson, *The Enlightenment,* p. 269.

Chapter 7: The Legacy of the Enlightenment

85. Kramnick, *The Portable Enlightenment Reader,* p. xvi.

86. Kramnick, ed., *The Portable Enlightenment Reader,* p. ix.

87. Nicolson, *The Age of Reason,* p. 14.

88. "Crimes of Reason," *Economist,* March 16, 1996.

89. Quoted in James Schmidt, ed., *What Is Enlightenment?: Eighteenth-Century Answers and Twentieth-Century Questions.* Berkeley and Los Angeles, University of California Press, 1996, p. 217.

90. Edward O. Wilson, "Back from Chaos," *Atlantic Monthly,* March 1998, p. 55.

For Further Reading

Susan Banfield, *The Rights of Man, the Reign of Terror: The Story of the French Revolution.* New York: J. B. Lippincott, 1989. A detailed, readable history of the French Revolution.

John Bowman, *The Age of Enlightenment.* New York: Golden Press, 1966. A readable volume that explains the key intellectual, scientific, political, and social ideas of the Enlightenment and the century that preceded it.

Trevor Cairns, *The Old Regime and the Revolution.* Minneapolis: Lerner, 1980. A concise and heavily illustrated history of eighteenth-century Europe.

Phyllis Corzine, *The French Revolution.* San Diego: Lucent Books, 1995. A well-written account of the French Revolution with many illustrations and extended quotes.

Peter Gay and the Editors of Time-Life Books, *Age of Enlightenment.* New York: Time-Life, 1966. An illustrated, readable, and concise history of the Enlightenment for the general reader.

Harry Henderson and Lisa Yount, *The Scientific Revolution.* San Diego: Lucent Books, 1996. A well-illustrated and readable account of the great scientific discoveries of the seventeenth and eighteenth centuries.

Christopher Hibber, ed., *Twilight of Princes.* New York: Newsweek Books, 1974. A collection of articles on eighteenth-century history, supplemented with colorful illustrations.

Works Consulted

M. H. Abrams, ed., *The Norton Anthology of English Literature.* Vol. 1. New York: W. W. Norton, 1968. A university-level anthology of British literature from the Middle Ages through the eighteenth century.

Isaiah Berlin, *The Age of Enlightenment: The 18th Century Philosophers.* New York: New American Library, 1956. Selections by eighteenth-century philosophers along with an introduction and commentary by a leading scholar on the Enlightenment.

John M. Blum et al., *The National Experience: A History of the United States.* 6th ed. San Diego: Harcourt Brace Jovanovich, 1985. A college-level textbook.

Louis I. Bredvold, *The Brave New World of the Enlightenment.* Ann Arbor: University of Michigan Press, 1961. A collection of six lectures given by the author on the Enlightenment at St. Olaf College in Northfield, Minnesota.

Henry Steele Commager, *The Empire of Reason: How Europe Imagined and America Realized the Enlightenment.* Garden City, NY: Anchor Press/Doubleday, 1977. An academic yet accessible work on the Enlightenment's impact on the development of America by a renowned historian.

"Crimes of Reason," *Economist.* March 16, 1996. An English periodical focusing on international economic and societal issues.

Lester G. Crocker, ed., *The Age of Enlightenment.* New York: Walker, 1969. A collection of writings by the philosophes.

Democracy in Germany: History and Perspectives. Published by the Press and Information Office of the Federal Government, Federal Republic of Germany. n.d. A government publication that traces the development of democracy in Germany.

Will and Ariel Durant, *The Age of Reason Begins.* Vol. VII of *The Story of Civilization.* New York: Simon and Schuster, 1961. A lively and interesting history of Europe from 1558 to 1648.

——, *The Age of Louis XIV.* Vol. VIII of *The Story of Civilization.* New York: Simon and Schuster, 1963. Next in a series covering civilization from 1648–1715.

——, *The Age of Voltaire.* Vol. IX of *The Story of Civilization.* New York: Simon and Schuster, 1965. This volume covers 1715 to 1756 with a focus on the conflict between religion and philosophy.

——, *Rousseau and Revolution.* Vol. X of *The Story of Civilization.* New York: Simon and Schuster, 1967. A history of European civilization from 1715 to 1789.

John A. Garraty and Peter Gay, eds., *The Columbia History of the World.* New York: Harper & Row, 1972. A concise, scholarly history of the world.

Peter Gay, *The Enlightenment: An Interpretation. Vol. 2, The Science of Freedom.* New York: Knopf, 1969. A scholarly work by a prize-winning author.

E. M. Halliday, "Nature's God and the Founding Fathers," *American Heritage.* New York: American Heritage, 1963.

Norman Hampson, *The Enlightenment.* Baltimore: Penguin Books, 1968. A scholarly history of the Enlightenment.

Ulrich Im Hof, *The Enlightenment.* trans. William E. Yuill. Oxford: Blackwell, 1994. An interesting and very readable history of the Enlightenment for both general readers and scholars.

Steven L. Jantzen, Larry S. Krieger, and Kenneth Neill, *World History: Perspectives on the Past.* Lexington, MA: D. C. Heath, 1992. A high school text filled with primary sources.

Isaac Kramnick, ed., *The Portable Enlightenment Reader.* New York: Penguin Books, 1995. A hefty anthology of primary sources from the Enlightenment.

T. Z. Lavine, *From Socrates to Sartre: The Philosophic Quest.* New York: Bantam, 1984. A popularized history of Western philosophy.

Frank E. Manuel, ed., *The Enlightenment.* Englewood Cliffs, NJ: Prentice-Hall, 1965. A collection of essays by a variety of philosophes.

Arthur J. May, *A History of Civilization: The Story of Our Heritage.* Vol. 2, *The Mid–Seventeenth Century to Modern Times.* New York: Charles Scribner's Sons, 1964. Enlightenment for the general reader. A compact history of the Enlightenment.

William H. McNeil, *The Rise of the West.* Chicago: University of Chicago Press, 1963. A scholarly history of Western civilization's rise to prominence in modern times.

Harold Nicolson, *The Age of Reason: The Eighteenth Century.* Garden City, NY: Doubleday, 1960. A scholarly yet very readable account of the major characters and issues of the Enlightenment.

Peyton E. Richter and Ilona Ricardo, *Voltaire.* Boston: Twayne, 1980. A scholarly but readable and fascinating look at the life and works of Voltaire.

James R. Rogers, "Faith and/or Reason," *National Review,* August 20, 1990. A summary of a critique of the Enlightenment by conservative intellectuals.

Jean-Jacques Rousseau, *The Social Contract.* Danbury, CT: Classics Appreciation Society, a Division of Grolier, 1957. A condensation of Rousseau's classic work.

Bertrand Russell, *Wisdom of the West.* London: Crescent Books, 1978. A historical survey of Western philosophy by a leading philosopher.

James Schmidt, ed., *What Is Enlightenment?: Eighteenth-Century Answers and Twentieth-Century Questions.* Berkeley and Los Angeles: University of California Press, 1996. A scholarly work comprising essays written by both philosophes and modern scholars.

Isidor Schneider, ed., *The Enlightenment: The Culture of the Eighteenth Century.* New York: George Braziller, 1965. A collection of writings from the Enlightenment edited by a leading scholar.

George Seldes, ed., *The Great Thoughts.* New York: Ballantine, 1985. A compilation of quoted material of many of history's most influential people.

Walter T. Wallbank, Alastair M. Taylor, and George Barr Carson Jr., *Civilization: Past and Present.* Chicago: Scott, Foresman, 1965. An exceptionally readable college-level textbook.

H. G. Wells, *The Outline of History.* Vol. 2. Garden City, NY: Garden City Books, 1920. A brief, readable history of humanity by a well-known popular writer.

Edward O. Wilson, "Back from Chaos," *Atlantic Monthly*, March 1998. A scholarly article on the Enlightenment by a renowned scholar.

Index

Picture Credits

About the Author

John M. Dunn is a freelance writer and high school history teacher. He has taught in Georgia, Florida, North Carolina, and Germany. As a writer and journalist, he has published over 250 articles and stories in more than 20 periodicals, as well as scripts for audio-visual productions and a children's play. His books—*The Russian Revolution, The Relocation of the North American Indian, The Spread of Islam, Advertising, The Civil Rights Movement*—are published by Lucent Books. He lives with his wife and two daughters in Ocala, Florida.